I0529116

MURDERED IN A HOODIE

A Forensic Autopsy
of the Evidence
Related to the Killing
of

Trayvon Martin

Co-Authors:

J. Cheney Mason

William R. Anderson, M.D.

1

This book is a work of nonfiction and presents an independent analysis of the events surrounding the death of Trayvon Martin, based on publicly available legal documents, forensic evidence, media reports, and expert commentary.

The views and opinions expressed are those of the authors based on their professional expertise and years of experience acquired from over fifty years of experience each and are intended solely for educational, informational, and analytical purposes. They do not constitute legal, medical, or forensic advice and should not be relied upon as such. The authors and publisher disclaim any losses or damages arising from the use of this book. Readers are encouraged to consult appropriate professionals for any legal or forensic interpretations or questions.

Published by Buster Bodhi Press
BusterBodhiPress.com

ISBN: 979-8-9991504-4-8
Library of Congress Control Number: 2025916186
Cover and Book Design: Mark Andrew James Terry
Editor: Joseph Cavanaugh
Printed in the United States of America

PROLOGUE

This book is an historic and analytical examination of one of the most important events in American society in the 21st century. Two of the world's most experienced experts in criminal law and forensic pathology have completed an exhaustive investigation into the fatal shooting of Black teenager Trayvon Martin in 2012, the subsequent judicial treatment of the man who pulled the trigger, George Zimmerman, and the birth of the Black Lives Matter (BLM) movement. This carefully researched and meticulously documented work takes the reader on a deep dive into the reality of Social Justice in America today.

Social Justice is the principle that all individuals and groups should receive fair treatment and equitable opportunities within our society. It is based on the United States Constitution that promises freedom and justice for all American citizens. Social Justice encompasses fairness and equity under our laws ensuring that all members of our society have the same rights and protection under the law.

The turmoil created by the events surrounding the murder of Trayvon Martin and the subsequent acquittal of George Zimmerman created the Black Lives Matter movement that continues today to be a major force advocating for racial justice and police accountability. The movement has been instrumental in pushing for legal reforms and raising awareness about the deeply rooted problem of systematic racism.

The Black Lives Matter movement has had social and political impacts, influencing public policy, and political activism nationwide. It has heightened awareness of systematic racism and the need for police reform, leading to widespread discussions on racial justice. It has had an impact on the media, the entertainment industry, and corporate policies. It has also influenced elections, mobilizing voters, particularly in minority communities, impacting local and national elections.

It has also spawned the White Lives Matter movement as a counter force in communities across the country. But really, can't we agree that all lives matter and that our country was founded on the principles of liberty and justice for all? This book points out that we need judicial reform and a return to the founding ideals that promise all citizens of this great nation equal rights to life, liberty, and the pursuit of happiness.

**This book is dedicated to
the pursuit of the truth — Forensic Science
in the courtroom**

ACKNOWLEDGMENTS

I wish to acknowledge the irreplaceable research and preparation of the manuscript and behind the scenes work of our associates on the project, Ms. Diana Marku and Ms. Virginia Poe, without whose help, I could not have brought this important document to fruition.

— J. Cheney Mason

I would like to acknowledge my wife and family who have been supportive throughout the endeavor and Drs. Page Hudson and Thomas Noguchi for instilling the concepts of the proper utilization of scientific factual evidence into the legal system, despite the often-encountered resistance of the latter to its realities in their adversarial environment.

— William R. Anderson, M.D.

TABLE OF CONTENTS

PREAMBLE

A Black teenager went to a convenience store to buy some Skittles and an iced tea. He was walking alone back to his father's condominium where he was visiting. He was confronted by an unknown man in plain clothes. Something happened between the two of them and the teenage boy was shot and killed. The shooter gave the first of many versions of his story to the police as to why he killed this innocent teenager.

During the immediate investigation, and continuing to today, the shooter changed his story repeatedly. Fiction became facts, facts disappeared.

Since that shooting on February 26, 2012, there has been substantial and continuing inquiry about what really did or did not happen. This book is intended to help our readers learn what truly did or did not happen and at least have informed information based on carefully researched facts.

The authors of this book have literally spent thousands of hours in research to come to the ultimate conclusion: at the trial the jury properly acquitted the shooter because the prosecution dramatically, and through incompetence, failed to present an accurate description of what actually occurred on that night.

The records reflect that the crime scene was mishandled from the very beginning. The law enforcement personnel totally failed to fully examine the crime scene and did apparently nothing to preserve its condition.

In addition to the law enforcement failures, the Medical Examiner basically failed to correctly analyze and interpret the forensic evidentiary data. Obvious available forensic evidence was ignored. No effort was made to locate, much less analyze evidence that would have and should have been available if the crime scene had been handled professionally based upon standard operating procedures.

The details of these failures and lack of competence are expertly analyzed by the authors and presented in this book.

Following the failure to properly gain, analyze, and understand the forensic evidence, the Prosecution was apparently oblivious to the necessary efforts they should have taken in pursuit of the truth. The authors believe that had this case been handled properly, the verdict may well have been different.

The authors, forensic pathologist Dr. Bill Anderson and attorney Cheney Mason, each have over 50 years of experience in dealing specifically with our legal system, evidence, forensics, and investigations of murder cases.

Dr. Anderson is a renowned medical examiner and pathologist having performed more than seven thousand autopsies. As medical director for a residency program training future forensic pathologists, he supervised fifteen hundred more autopsies and attended and analyzed hundreds of crime scene investigations as a Medical Examiner.

Mr. Mason is a nationally recognized Board-Certified criminal trial lawyer expert. He tried his first homicide criminal defense case over 50 years ago in 1972 and has been a key defense lawyer in more than three hundred and fifty jury trials.

Dr. Anderson and Mr. Mason have reviewed all the available court documents, records, and related transcripts. They have carefully analyzed all forensic reports and the autopsy of the victim, Trayvon Martin.

In addition to their comprehensive analysis of trial records and police documents, the authors have reviewed over eleven thousand publicly reported news accounts from more than fifteen sources that daily covered the trial.

These two highly experienced experts have carefully studied the undisputed records of the relevant legal presentations and forensic evidence to create this comprehensive analysis of the unforgettable events which resulted in the death of Trayvon Martin.

Chapter One

1

THE MURDER

He was only seventeen years old. He had a youthful looking face that made him appear even younger. Trayvon had been living with his mother in Miami Gardens and was used to a more crowded, urban neighborhood. He had come to this small, rural, old southern town, Sanford, Florida, to spend some time visiting with his father. His father had recently moved into a new upscale, gated apartment development.

On this late February afternoon, he decided to walk from his father's apartment to a nearby convenience store, only a couple of blocks away. He wanted some Skittles and an Arizona Iced Tea.

It was late in the afternoon and getting dark early as it was the end of February. He walked to the convenience store, bought his Skittles and tea, and walked back to his father's apartment. His path from his father's apartment to the nearby convenience store and back was on paved sidewalks through landscaped areas and the middle of the courtyard of this new development.

His route was fully open and available for view by anybody in the area. His path took him between apartment buildings that were two stories tall and anybody walking on these open sidewalks could be seen by dozens of people in the adjacent apartments. The walkways went by the front entrances of most of these homes.

On this leisurely walk home from the convenience store, Trayvon had no way of knowing that he was under surveillance by a Neighborhood Watch volunteer, later determined to be George Zimmerman. As he walked through the complex, returning to his father's home, while on the phone with his girlfriend he told her that he was being followed by some "cracker." Trayvon did not know what was about to happen to him as he was innocently walking back to his father's apartment.

He was concerned about a man who was approaching him. He told his girlfriend in Miami that he was being followed and did not know why or what was going on. The next thing she heard was Trayvon screaming for help.

Trayvon had no way of knowing that only moments before being confronted by the "cracker" that this individual had called the police department to report a suspicious character in the neighborhood. Apparently, the teen appeared suspicious because he was a young, Black male wearing a hoodie.

The police department recordings revealed that Zimmerman said that he was observing a "suspicious person" in the neighborhood and was going to follow him. He further told the police that a lot of burglaries had been in the area lately and was heard to say, in the recording, that "these assholes, they always get away." He further indicated that he was going to follow the suspect, and was told by the 911 operator, "Not to do it."

12

Racial issues become a factor in George Zimmerman murder trial

BY RENE STUTZMAN
Staff writer

SANFORD — It was a startling moment at George Zimmerman's murder trial: Defense attorney Don West suggested that Trayvon Martin — not the defendant — was guilty of racial bias the night the two met on a rainy Sanford sidewalk and Zimmerman shot the black teenager dead.

Martin had described Zimmerman as a "creepy-ass cracker" to his friend Rachel Jeantel, who was on the phone with him in the moments before the shooting, she testified.

"Trayvon Martin referred to white people as crackers, correct?" West asked the 19-year-old woman.

"I don't recall, sir," she said. But moments earlier she had confirmed that he had.

In a case that became a national civil-rights cause celebre — drawing thousands of protesters, the Rev. Al Sharpton and the Rev. Jesse Jackson to Sanford — there have been surprisingly few direct references to race or racism at Zimmerman's trial.

The issue of race, though, is never far from the surface.

Thursday's confrontation between West and Jeantel was one example.

George Ciccariello-Maher, a professor of history and politics at Drexel University in Philadelphia, said from Martin's choice of words on the phone that night, it appeared that "he perceived intuitively" that Zimmerman's following him was a "racial pursuit."

Martin didn't inject race into what happened that night, Ciccariello-Maher argued. He used the phrase "cracker" pejoratively to

JOE BURBANK/STAFF PHOTOGRAPHER
Issues of race were raised Thursday when witness Rachel Jeantel testified that Trayvon Martin referred to murder defendant George Zimmerman as a "creepy-ass cracker." Zimmerman is Hispanic.

describe someone already acting with racial motives.

Injecting race

Martin's death became the top news story in the country in March 2012 when more than a million people signed a petition, outraged that Zimmerman — who many believed is white but who is a light-skinned Hispanic — had shot an unarmed black 17-year-old in a gated community and not been arrested.

After court Thursday — when race surfaced in testimony — Daryl Parks, an attorney for Martin's parents, stood alongside them in a news conference to say: "To this family, race is not a part of this process. Anybody who tries to inject it is wrong."

And yet, Martin's parents traveled to Washington, D.C., where the Congressional Black Caucus described the killing as one of "racial bias."

There were rallies in New York, Los Angeles, London, Chicago, Atlanta, Denver, Detroit, Toronto, Miami and elsewhere.

Thousands thronged to Sanford for rallies led by the Jackson and Sharpton, who warned that without an arrest, Sanford was "risking going down as the Birmingham and Selma of the 21st century."

U.S. Rep. Corrine Brown helped persuade the U.S. Department of Justice to launch an investigation to determine whether Zimmerman had violated Martin's civil rights. The agency has not announced its conclusions.

Skin color issue

The defense has been saying all along that Martin's skin color was not a factor in the confrontation and shooting. At the close of testimony Friday, Shawn Vincent, spokesman for Zimmerman's attorneys, said about the case: "We

don't think it's about race."

Yet race has surfaced in court.

It became an issue Wednesday when prosecutors persuaded Circuit Judge Debra S. Nelson to allow them to play for jurors five recorded phone calls Zimmerman, a Neighborhood Watch volunteer, had made to police in the months leading up to the Feb. 26, 2012, shooting.

In four of those calls, he was reporting suspicious persons in his neighborhood. Each time, the person was black.

Assistant State Attorney Richard Mantei had argued that the tapes would help jurors understand Zimmerman's motive the night of the shooting: Zimmerman was tired of suspicious people in his neighborhood and believed "these assholes, they always get away," words he used with a dispatcher the night he called to report Martin.

During opening statements, the judge allowed Assistant State Attorney

John Guy to accuse Zimmerman of profiling — but not to say "racial profiling."

The most overt reference to race came Thursday from Jeantel. When asked, she told West she believed the killing was racial because of the way Martin described Zimmerman, as a "creepy-ass cracker." She did not explain.

Even in choosing the jury, race was a factor. The panel is all women, five white and one Hispanic. If not for defense challenges, two of the three white alternates would be black.

"That is not a jury that will be able to deliver a fair verdict," Ciccariello-Maher said.

Defense attorney Mark O'Mara made no apology for using his challenges to excuse two black women from the jury. He had played by the rules, he said.

Parks, one of the attorneys for Martin's family, said he was not worried that the jury has five white members and one Hispanic. The case, he has often said, is about justice for Martin.

Regarding race, Parks said, "America doesn't want to talk about that."

rstutzman@tribune.com

Obituaries

Broward County

Becraft
Becraft, Brent,43,of Boynton Beach, [...] accident June 28,2012. Fred Hunte[...] Funeral Home, University Dr Davie

Hyatt

13

TRAYVON MARTIN SHOOTING

Trayvon on phone just before he died

• SHOOTING, FROM 1A

Attorney Norm Wolfinger announced he would convene a grand jury next month to probe the case, which is now being reviewed by the U.S. Department of Justice Civil Rights Division, the FBI and the Florida Department of Law Enforcement.

With the case becoming a national cause célèbre and racial tempers flaring, social media sites were exploding Tuesday

TRAYVON

with the belief that the teen's killer used a racial epithet just minutes before he shot Trayvon.

George Zimmerman, 28, an aspiring police officer who once attended a citizen police academy, called Sanford Police on Feb. 26 to report a suspicious person in his gated townhouse complex. It was one of the dozens of times he had called police over the years, and one of several where he called to report the presence of a black male.

After the shooting, Zimmerman told police the young man came at him from behind and attacked him and he fired in self-defense. He was not charged, triggering national outrage and an online petition that drew more than 600,000 signatures.

On the recording of his call to police that is posted on the city's website, Zimmerman can be heard breathing heavily as he pursued Trayvon through the complex. Then, about two minutes into the call, under his breath, he used a profanity and a second word that sounded like a racial slur, but it was nearly inaudible and difficult to decipher.

Like the scores of news agencies that had listened to the tape over and over since it was released Friday, Sanford Police spokesman Sgt.

JACQUELYN MARTIN/AP

IN WASHINGTON: Sanford City Manager Norton Bonapart Jr., left, speaks to, from left, U.S. Rep. Corrine Brown, D-Jacksonville; Sanford Mayor Jeff Triplett, and U.S. Rep. Frederica Wilson, D-Miami.

David Morgenstern said no one at the police department had noticed the muttering before Tuesday.

"I listened to that tape several times, and I never heard it before," he said. "I am quite sure the grand jury will listen to it."

Benjamin Crump, the attorney for the dead teen's family, said the incident was another disturbing development in a case riddled with police missteps. He was also troubled by the decision to take the case to a grand jury, which meets in private.

If the roles had been reversed, "Would Trayvon Martin have gotten the courtesy of a grand jury?" Crump said. "Whatever case they put out, we won't know. They can come out, wipe their hands clean like Pontius Pilate and say 'It wasn't us; it was the community.' "

Crump, who is based in Tallahassee, flew to Miami after Trayvon's father combed through his son's

cellphone records and discovered he was on the telephone just moments before he died.

The number belonged to a girl Trayvon had spent hours talking to that weekend, a girl he was dating. Crump recorded her statement and played it for reporters at a press conference in Fort Lauderdale Tuesday, but said he promised the girl's parents he would not reveal her name.

Records show she called Trayvon at 7:12 p.m., and spoke to him for four minutes. Zimmerman's call to police was at 7:11.

She told Crump that Trayvon said he was being followed.

"Run!" she recalled telling him. "Trayvon said he's not running."

Crump said phone records back up the girl's story, showing that the "suspicious" person who neighborhood watch thought was "up to no good" was simply a teen like any other — one who ran up 400 minutes that weekend talking on his cell.

"This girl connects the dots," said Crump, who added he plans to turn the tape over to federal investigators, but not to Sanford police.

Morgenstern, the Sanford police spokesman, said the department had urged anyone with information to come forward, and the girl who was talking to Trayvon that night never did.

"We are open to the U.S.

JOE RAEDLE/GETTY IMAGES

MARTIN FAMILY ATTORNEY: Benjamin Crump holds cellphone records showing Trayvon's final call.

Department of Justice and the FDLE to come take a look our investigation, pick it apart, criticize it and let us know how we did," he said. "We think we've done the best and fairest investigation we could."

On Tuesday, members of the Congressional Black Caucus in Washington, D.C. — joined by Sanford's mayor — met with senior Justice Department officials, including the head of the civil rights division, Thomas Perez, to talk about Trayvon's death.

"I am tired of burying black boys," said Rep. Frederica Wilson, D-Miami. "I can't even explain how sad this makes me."

In Tallahassee, state Attorney General Pam Bondi

said "no stone will be left unturned in this investigation."

Attorneys for Trayvon's family accuse the Sanford police of protecting Zimmerman because he shares their love for law enforcement.

Zimmerman, who was born in Virginia and studied criminal justice at Seminole State College, is the son of a retired Virginia Supreme Court magistrate and his wife, a long time clerk of courts, according to his application to the citizen's police academy.

Sanford police released a log of Zimmerman's dozens of calls to police dating back to 2004, which show a pattern of his reporting suspicious people and minor nuisances. Three other reports

released by the county sheriff show Zimmerman was willing to follow wrong-doers.

In September 2003, Zimmerman called police to complain of a fellow motorist spitting on him. He followed the man until police arrived.

But the motorist, Daniel Osmun, told police that Zimmerman was tailgating and he spit his gum out the window "out of frustration" with the young man's erratic driving.

As they pulled up next to each other, the two exchanged words and "Mr. Osmun

ZIMMERMAN

also said at one point, he thought Mr. Zimmerman was going to attack him," according to a police report. Prosecutors were contacted but no charges were ever filed against either, according to state records.

In October 2003, Zimmerman again called police as he followed a man who had apparently stolen two combination DVD/TV players from a supermarket. The suspected thief was arrested.

Then in October 2007, Zimmerman called police to report that the tires of his Dodge Durango had been slashed and he suspected his girlfriend's ex-boyfriend. However, he had no proof the man, Tim Hudik, was behind the vandalism.

Hudik told police that he never touched the truck — and that he was so aggravated by text message exchanges with Zimmerman that he was mulling a restraining order against Zimmerman.

None was filed, according to Seminole County records.

Hudik hung up on a Miami Herald reporter Tuesday.

Zimmerman was arrested in a scuffle with an undercover officer in 2005, but the charges were dropped when he entered a pre-trial diversion program that allowed him to have a clean record.

When he applied for the citizen's police academy, Zimmerman insisted he did not know the man he scuffled with was a cop.

"I hold law enforcement officers in the highest regaurd [sic] as I hope to one day become one," he wrote in his application.

"I would never have touched a police officer."

14

TRAYVON

Continued from **Page A1**

merman's statements include that allegation. But authorities do not think that happened, the source told the Sentinel, because on one 911 call, someone can be heard screaming for help. If it were Zimmerman, as he claims, his cries were not muffled, the source said.

Zimmerman also told police, the source told the Sentinel, that while the two were on the ground, Trayvon reached for Zimmerman's gun, and the two struggled over it. Those portions of Zimmerman's account are not corroborated by other evidence, the source said.

Zimmerman's attorney, Mark O'Mara, said he hasn't yet seen his client's statements to police, and it would be inappropriate for him to address specific evidence in the case.

"It's hard for me to even comment on it," O'Mara said.

Sanford police spokesman Sgt. David Morgenstern said the Police Department "cannot make any comments on anything related to the George Zimmerman/Trayvon Martin case."

Reached in Birmingham, Ala., Martin family attorney Benjamin Crump said Thursday that Zimmerman's claims that he was screaming in the 911 call and that his mouth was covered by the teen don't add up.

"[Trayvon's father] Tracy Martin told me that that's what [police] told him," Crump said of Zimmerman making those statements to police.

"It's either one or the other — it can't be both," Crump said. "We have to put together this puzzle because, unfortunately, we don't have Trayvon Martin's version" of events.

A spokeswoman for Special Prosecutor Angela Corey would not comment.

Zimmerman is charged with second-degree murder in the shooting death of Trayvon in a Sanford gated community Feb. 26. Zimmerman told police he acted in self-defense. Critics say he is guilty of racial profiling and killing an innocent teenager.

In an audio recording of Zimmerman's call to police that night, Zimmerman says Trayvon is acting suspiciously and describes him as a black teenager when prompted by the dispatcher. He does not say that Trayvon was circling his vehicle, but that's what he told police later that night and has consistently told authorities in subsequent interviews, according to the Sentinel's source.

Here, according to that source, is the sequence that Zimmerman provided:

Zimmerman spotted Trayvon, called a nonemergency police number and began describing the teenager. While he was doing that, Trayvon came toward his vehicle and began to circle it.

Zimmerman, though, never described

> "We have to put together this puzzle because . . . we don't have Trayvon Martin's version."
>
> *Benjamin Crump, Martin family attorney*

that to the dispatcher.

At one point, about halfway through the four-minute call, he told the dispatcher, "Now he's just staring at me. ... Now he's coming towards me. He's got his hand in his waistband. ... He's coming to check me out."

Trayvon then disappeared, Zimmerman later told authorities, according to the source, and while Zimmerman was still on the phone, he parked his vehicle, got out and began trying to find Trayvon on foot.

Zimmerman can be heard huffing and puffing on the call to police.

"Are you following him?" the dispatcher asks.

"Yeah," Zimmerman said.

"We don't need you to do that," the dispatcher says.

Zimmerman later told investigators he could not find Trayvon, so he turned and walked back toward his SUV. A short time later, Trayvon approached from the rear, and they exchanged words, he told authorities.

Trayvon threw the first punch, he told police. It knocked Zimmerman to the ground, and the teenager then got on top of Zimmerman and began beating his head against a sidewalk, police have said in recounting Zimmerman's version of events.

At an April 20 bail hearing in Sanford, Dale Gilbreath, an investigator for Corey, testified that Zimmerman told authorities he was frightened because Trayvon circled him while he sat in his SUV.

Gilbreath described that as one of the inconsistencies in Zimmerman's story — because getting out of the vehicle and looking for the teen is not the act of someone who is afraid.

Gilbreath did not testify that Zimmerman claimed the circling happened while he was on the phone with the dispatcher.

Gilbreath also testified briefly about Zimmerman telling police that Trayvon had his hand over Zimmerman's mouth in the fight.

Several audio experts who have analyzed the 911 tapes for the Sentinel and other news outlets have said they think it is Trayvon's voice — not Zimmerman's — crying out for help. However, Gilbreath testified that similar identification attempts by law enforcement were fruitless.

rstutzman@tribune.com or 407-650-6394
jeweiner@tribune.com or 407-420-5151

World briefing

Tribune Newspapers and news services

NBC: 'We deeply regret' edits on Sanford 911 call

NBC News apologized Tuesday for the way it edited a broadcast of a conversation between George Zimmerman and a police dispatcher before Trayvon Martin was killed in Sanford, Fla.

Last week, Fox News did a report in which it presented "before" and "after" versions of the call. NBC had broadcast the edited exchange on its "Today" show. NBC News launched an investigation after the Fox report.

"During our investigation it became evident that there was an error made in the production process that we deeply regret," NBC News representative Lauren Kapp said in a statement Tuesday. "We will be taking the necessary steps to prevent this from happening in the future and apologize to our viewers."

The issue of the edited call in NBC and MSNBC news stories was raised on right-leaning blogs that monitor the media. NBC News first responded to queries Thursday, Kapp said. Over the weekend it told a Washington Post blog it would investigate its handling of the piece.

The "Today" show's segment, which included an ellipsis on screen to indicate omitted text, ran as:

"Zimmerman: 'This guy looks like he's up to no good ...'

"Zimmerman: 'He looks black.' "

The full conversation ran as:

"Zimmerman: 'This guy looks like he's up to no good. Or he's on drugs or something. It's raining and he's just walking around, looking about.'

"Dispatcher: 'OK, and this guy — is he black, white or Hispanic?'

"Zimmerman: 'He looks black.' "

16

He told the 911 operator that he was going to follow the suspect and was told directly by the dispatcher: "You don't need to do that!" He chose to intentionally disregard the direct command. By doing so Mr. Zimmerman violated the rules of the Neighborhood Watch Guidelines.

The lead detective involved in this case stated that if Mr. Zimmerman had in fact advised this young man that he was with the Neighborhood Watch, it is most likely that there would never have been a trial because there never would have been any assault and shooting.

The 11:00 Sunday evening news was interrupted by the announcement of "breaking news" referencing a shooting that had just taken place in a condominium complex in Sanford, Florida.

According to the first television news accounts, the shooting had taken place earlier in the evening and that it resulted in at least one fatality—although details were sketchy at that point and the situation was under active law-enforcement investigation.

The initial news reports lit the fire of racism that rampantly spread throughout the nation. According to the broadcast, Mr. Zimmerman was quoted as saying that "The guy looks like he is up to no good, he looks Black." Immediately, there was an NBC broadcast recording purporting to be Zimmerman's 911 call of the incident. This of course fanned the fire that spread.

What he actually said was that, according to the 911 call, "This guy looks like he is up to no good, or he is on drugs or something. It's raining and he is just walking around looking about." At this point the dispatcher for the police department stated, "Okay and this guy, is he black, white, or Hispanic?" Zimmerman, in a response said, "He looks Black."

From that point on the journalists treated it as an undisputed fact the suspicious person was Black and that may have had something to do with the response by the Neighborhood Watch volunteer. As we now know, a similar misleading allegation was broadcast by a local radio station. They and another TV station falsely and obviously intentionally exacerbated the alleged "racial" issue and even broadcast knowingly false photographs of a young Black man flipping the camera the bird with his underwear exposed. As we now know and learned very quickly back then, that was not a photograph of Trayvon Martin.

Zimmerman had not initially asserted that he was Black, only responding to the option presented by the police. Both NBC and the other copying radio and TV stations had to print retractions of their allegations. In fact, there were lawsuits that followed because of the damage created by the malicious and false statements, and the journalists not only had to retract, but also pay significant damages.

There had been no complaints called in by any citizen, nor any apparent disturbance of any kind. The police on the recording advised Zimmerman not to follow the young man and that they were sending somebody to respond.

Trayvon, having just turned seventeen, was a young kid of slight frame. He weighed a little over one hundred and fifty pounds and his baby face appeared even younger. Trayvon had no way of knowing who this guy was or why he was following him. He had done nothing; he knew nobody in the area, except his father, who was in his apartment only a short distance away.

Zimmerman, a White man, was in recreational casual clothes without any official badge or visual security guard identification. He was armed with a pistol that was under his jacket which was probably not visible to Trayvon or apparently anybody else at that time. He ignored the directions from the police department to not follow the kid and did it anyway.

There had been no claim or complaint from any resident. There was no evidence of any break-in, property damage, vandalism, or anything that could be considered suspicious. The difference was apparently that this young kid was not known to Zimmerman, and he was Black. He was wearing what Zimmerman saw as a dangerous "disguise": a hooded jacket.

Some neighbors reported hearing what sounded like a youthful cry for help then a gun shot.

At least one other "ear witness", a nearby resident, heard the cry. The witness described it as probably male, but not sure. This evaluation later may be seen to have corroborated the fact that it was young Trayvon calling for help, not the voice of an adult.

The police, who had advised Zimmerman not to follow the kid, did indeed arrive at the scene within another minute. He had not followed the directions of the police. He asserted himself and, despite the warning, apparently followed this kid who had not done anything improper. The youthful Trayvon was lying on the ground with a bullet hole in his chest. The first responders rushed immediately to the scene and appropriately inquired as to what was going on.

They had a body; the body had a bullet hole; there was no apparent weapon, except the shooter's pistol, the literal smoking gun.

Zimmerman identified himself and thereafter claimed that he was the "commander" of security for this apartment project. This shooter was the epitome of what would later be characterized in several news articles as a "Wannabe."

Webster's Dictionary describes a Wannabe as "a person who wants or aspires to be someone or something else or who tries to look or act like someone else." In fact, as the investigation carried on, it turns out that this "watch commander" had been one of these people so obsessed with the power of law enforcement that he became an occasional "rider" with the police department. Many law enforcement agencies encouraged "riders" as a public relations effort. He had ridden with the police before and apparently enjoyed the

SANFORD SHOOTING

Witness: 'I heard a cry and a shot'

● WITNESSES, FROM 1A

In fear for his life, he pulled Kel Tek 9mm handgun from his waistband and shot.

From Facebook to Twitter and online petitions, local police and prosecutors are getting tens of thousands of demands for criminal charges as the national media shines a spotlight on a small, racially diverse central Florida town with a history of police tension. There are now more and more calls for the U.S. Department of Justice to intervene and try to answer: What really happened to Trayvon Martin?

'IT WAS A CHILD'

"I heard someone crying — not boo-hoo crying, but scared or terrified or hurt maybe," said Mary Cutcher, 31, who lives in the Retreat at Twin Lakes townhome community where the shooting occurred. "To me, it was a child."

Zimmerman said he tailed Trayvon in a mission to find out if the teen was up to no good. Zimmerman was out to put a stop to recent burglaries. He dialed police — his 46th call in the past 14 months to report shady people, reckless drivers and other disturbances around his neighborhood.

He offered to follow his suspect, but the dispatcher told him: "We don't need you to do that."

But Zimmerman did anyway. Some minutes later, Trayvon was killed with a gun the watch volunteer was licensed to carry.

"This was not self-defense," Cutcher said. "We heard no fighting, no wrestling, no punching. We heard a boy crying. As soon as the shot went off, it stopped, which tells me it was the child crying. If it had been Zimmerman crying, it wouldn't have stopped. If you're hurting, you're hurting."

She and her friend say they heard the sounds from a few steps away, where they were inside beside an open window.

Seconds later, they dashed out to find a boy face down on the ground and a man standing over him, a foot on each side of the body on the ground, with his hands pinning the shooting victim down.

"I asked him, 'What's happening here? What's going on?'" said Cutcher's friend, Selma Mora Lamilla. "The third time, I was indignant, and he said, 'just call the police.' Then I saw him with his hands over his head in the universal sign of: 'Oh man, I messed up.'"

The women, who were the first on the scene, said they saw Zimmerman pacing back and forth.

"I know what I heard. I heard a cry and a shot," Mora said.

"If there was a fight, it did not happen here where the boy was shot. I would have heard it, as this all happened right outside my open window."

The women think there may well have been a physical altercation between the two, but it must have taken place in a different spot.

Cutcher was one of eight or nine 911 callers that night but she said investigators dismissed her, and a detective failed to follow up with her.

"Mr. Zimmerman's claim is that the confrontation was initiated by Trayvon," Police Chief Bill Lee said in an interview. "I am not going into specifics of what led to the violent physical encounter witnessed by residents. All the physical evidence and testimony we have independent of what Mr. Zimmerman provides corroborates this claim to self-defense."

To claim self-defense, someone has to show there was danger of great bodily harm or death, Lee said. "Zimmerman had injuries consistent with his story," Lee said.

BLOODY WOUND

Zimmerman had a damp shirt, grass stains, a bloody nose and was bleeding from a wound in back of his head, according to police reports.

"If someone asks you, 'Hey do you live here?' is it OK for you to jump on them and beat the crap out of somebody?" Lee said. "It's not."

A neighborhood eighth-grader out walking his dog said his family also called 911.

"I saw someone lying on the ground, and I heard screaming," said Austin, 13, whose mother asked that his last name not be published. "I don't know that it was the person on the [ground] who was screaming, but to me it sounded like a kid who was crying. It was a yell for help, and I think it was Trayvon."

Austin wasn't sure if the person was in a fight or had slipped and gotten hurt. Austin's boxer puppy got off the leash so the boy went chasing after the dog and lost sight of the scene for a moment. Then, he heard a gun go off.

He ran home and told his sister to call the police.

The boy, who is black, has been rattled ever since. He feels angry and disconcerted, and wonders whether he's at risk too.

"That people can stereotype like that makes you scared," he said.

Austin's mom said he's been acting out in school and seems mad all the time.

"My son has a terrible feeling of guilt, because he did not do anything to help. He's angry," said Austin's mother, Cheryl Brown. "They are saying that Trayvon looked suspicious, because he was walking slow. So I guess I have to tell my son: make sure you always run fast."

Lee released a statement Thursday disputing Cutcher's account, saying it differed from what she originally told police, which she angrily denies.

Cutcher originally gave police a statement that matched Zimmerman's account, said police spokesman Sgt. David Morgenstern.

Sanford's Police Chief Lee is "asking the public and the media to give the system the opportunity to work, in the interest of safety of the community," Morgenstern said.

Zimmerman, whose whereabouts are unknown, was not charged, and the case is now under review by the Brevard Seminole state attorney's office.

Local and national black leaders have rallied around the incident as the latest example of a double standard of justice in what they consider a case of racial profiling.

DAD'S LETTER

On Thursday, Zimmerman's father hand-delivered a letter to the Orlando Sentinel, disputing widely repeated version of events, saying his Spanish-speaking son is not a racist.

"The media reports of the events are imaginary at best. At no time did George follow or confront Mr. Martin," Robert Zimmerman wrote. "When the true details of the event become public, and I hope that will be soon, everyone should be outraged by the treatment of George Zimmerman in the media."

A rally is planned for the Sanford City Council meeting March 26. Leaders are asking people to show up carrying Skittles, the candy Trayvon carried in his pocket when he died.

The witnesses say they are coming forward now because they were shocked when no arrest was made.

"They are protecting Zimmerman for some reason," Trayvon's mother Sybrina Fulton said in Miami. "They are protecting him and we feel that Trayvon is the victim."

Lee said the matter needs to be taken to a grand jury as soon as possible.

"If the roles were reversed, our investigation would be exactly the same," he said.

"Our investigation is color blind and based on the facts and circumstances, not color. I know I can say that until I am blue in the face, but as a white man in a uniform, I know it doesn't mean anything to anybody."

IN MY OPINION
Fabiola Santiago
fsantiago@MiamiHerald.com

Zimmerman star witness against self

It's too early in the George Zimmerman murder trial to make any predictions.

But at least one of the prevailing questions arising before the six-woman jury was seated and sequestered — can Zimmerman get a fair trial, given the high-profile status of the case and the excessive publicity surrounding it? — has been answered with a resounding "Yes."

For one, the neighborhood watchman's defense team has been exhaustingly aggressive in its cross-examination of every state witness, with enough success, it seems, to plant doubt and drive observers to question the prosecution's strategy and speculate that a second-degree murder conviction will be impossible for a jury to reach.

On Tuesday, defense attorney Mark O'Mara tried to keep out evidence that portrays Zimmerman as a wannabe cop whose zealotry led him to profile 17-year-old Trayvon Martin, who was returning on a rainy night from a trip to a 7-Eleven, as a potential criminal.

The evidence — college documents and a request to ride along with police officers — shows that Zimmerman was a criminal justice major who knew enough about Florida law to quickly come up with a self-defense story that would justify his use of deadly force against the unarmed Miami Gardens teen, who was staying with his father in the Sanford gated community where Zimmerman lived.

Judge Debra Nelson is scheduled to rule Wednesday about whether the jury will see the documents, which bolster the prosecution's contention that Zimmerman acted as a vigilante who profiled and followed Tray-

experience. He had gotten a license to carry a firearm, though he had no historical need or employment that justified it. It was legal and he seemed proud to be a legal gun owner.

Later, investigation would reveal that this watch commander had not only been a persistent "rider", he also had applied for employment as a police officer by the same police department but had been rejected.

As reported by numerous news "sources" when confronted by the police responders, the shooter offered an immediate explanation to try to explain the obvious, a dead body.

He claimed that he had been attacked for some unknown reason and that he had to defend himself.

He claimed that this slight teenager had overpowered him, a two-hundred-pound man, throwing him to the ground, and banging his head on the sidewalk.

He claimed that during this unprovoked melee, he had no choice but to defend himself and that the kid was reaching for the gun that he carried on his hip. The shooter then says that because the kid was trying to grab the gun, he "beat him to the draw" and had no choice but to shoot.

When initially talking with police, Zimmerman did claim that he had indeed "beat the kid to the draw", a term that one might easily visualize as a scene from an old cowboy movie with the winner of a gunfight raising his recently fired pistol up and blowing the smoke off the barrel in a gesture of victory.

When the police were initially questioning Mr. Zimmerman moments after the shooting and Zimmerman was recounting his story about what had happened, he began to make numerous changes to his story.

Significantly, after he had fired his gun, he was talking to the responding police officer then he coolly and very cavalierly said to the officer "Just call my wife and tell her I shot somebody."

It had begun to rain slightly. The resident "ear and potentially eyewitnesses" had not gathered around the scene yet; there hadn't been time. The police turned Trayvon's body over to lie with his face up and could see the hole in his chest and all the blood. The kid's hands were empty and there was nothing on or about his body except his iced tea, Skittles, and phone.

Zimmerman asserted that upon his immediate confrontation, the kid had, with no provocation, hit him in the face. He also claimed that as part of this physical confrontation that the kid instantly tried to reach over to Mr. Zimmerman's hip to grab his pistol.

This scenario, later reenacted by the shooter himself, on a recorded video, has some serious inconsistencies when compared to the actual forensics of the bullet shot and tra-

21

jectory through Trayvon Martin's body.

Zimmerman had a few sharp-edged lacerations on the posterior upper area of his scalp with some bleeding, but nowhere was the amount of blood consistent with lacerations to this highly vascularized area of the body. With the body lying there and the police looking around with their lights while they listened to Zimmerman's claims, no one apparently saw any blood, hair, or other material on the sidewalk where the reported slamming of his head allegedly occurred.

Furthermore, photos taken at the scene show that little effort was made to cover any of the involved areas in order to protect potentially critical physical forensic evidence that might shed further light on the train of events and serve to either corroborate or discredit Zimmerman's account of events.

Accounts from the Sheriff's department, as well as intake photos from the jail, indicate that the paramedics had spent at least some amount of time evaluating his wounds and rendering emergency medical care and treatment as reported in the Orlando Sentinel Friday March 20, 2012.

Ultimately, it was determined that the wounds in the head were not considered to be severe enough to require hospitalization.

The police began their investigation following an unheard-of procedure in the experience of your authors. They had a dead body, one armed guy, one gun, one shot heard, and the claim of self-defense. Zimmerman was not even officially arrested.

The video isn't the only new information that could contradict Zimmerman's account of the incident. The man who prepared the teenager's body for burial also doubts his story.

Richard Kurtz, a funeral director for Roy Mizell and Kurtz Funeral Home in Fort Lauderdale, says that when he heard of Zimmerman's self-defense claim in the media, "it did not add up."

"I did not see any signs that would indicate to me that [Trayvon] was beating anybody," Kurtz told the Orlando Sentinel. "He just looked like a normal person that got shot."

Kurtz said he would have expected bruising or cuts on the teen's hands or body but saw none. When he heard Zimmerman was claiming he had been punched by Trayvon, "the story did not fit the situation."

Zimmerman fatally shot Trayvon, an unarmed black 17-year-old from Miami Gardens, on Feb. 26 in the Retreat at Twin Lakes, a gated subdivision where Zimmerman lived.

Zimmerman, who said he shot the teen in self-defense, has not been charged with a crime. The shooting has sparked international outrage. Zimmerman is currently in hiding — his father Robert Zimmerman told the Orlando Sentinel the family has received death threats.

Police say Zimmerman, who is 5-foot-9, told them he shot Trayvon in self-defense after the high-school junior, described in a police report as 6 feet tall and 160 pounds, attacked and beat him.

The police report says Zimmerman was bleeding from his nose and head when officers arrived. He was tended by paramedics but told them he did not need to go to a hospital, police reported.

The Orlando Sentinel (Orlando, Florida) · Fri, Mar 30, 2012 · Page A8

22

Chapter Two

MEDICAL EXAMINER'S INVOLVEMENT

In the state of Florida, any death that occurs that is traumatic, violent, suspicious, or sudden and unexpected potentially comes under the jurisdiction of the Medical Examiner's office in the district in which the death was believed to have taken place.

In 2012, the County of Seminole, including the city of Sanford, was part of the jurisdiction of the Volusia County Medical Examiner under a contractual arrangement entered into several years earlier to provide forensic investigative services as a "cost-saving" arrangement in lieu of maintaining their own medical examiner's office as was the case in most other large metropolitan jurisdictions. This even though the Volusia County office was geographically separated from much of populated Seminole County by at least forty miles, making timely responses to death scenes impossible.

Under most circumstances, death investigations are relatively routine and don't require immediate input from trained forensic personnel. In situations that are suspicious, unusual or have some element of traumatic injury involved, immediate analysis of a victim may become critical in determining such things as cause of death, time of death, potential activities of the victim following the infliction of the injury.

Of equal importance is the proper collection and preservation of trace evidence that could turn out to be critical as well in the final determination as to the manner of death— whether it be accidental, natural, suicide or homicide.

Obviously, this can create a real problem if there are significant geographic challenges preventing an immediate response. While law-enforcement personnel may have sufficient expertise to evaluate a crime scene, they are in no way qualified to make the medical forensic determinations upon which the ultimate outcome of a case may hinge.

This was the situation that existed on the evening of February 26, 2012, in the courtyard behind the condominium at 2861 Retreat View Circle where the body of a then unidentified Black male was lying on the grass—the victim of an apparent gunshot wound to the chest.

According to recordings and witness interviews regarding the initial investigation, the shooting occurred at or about 7:20 PM with law enforcement arriving on the scene within a few minutes afterwards.

Paramedics subsequently made a pronouncement of death at about 7:30 PM as reflected in the Medical Examiner Investigation Records.

Review of the records from the Volusia County Medical Examiner's Office, indicates that their office was notified of the death at 8:32 PM, and that Forensic Investigator Malphurs did not actually arrive at the scene in Sanford until 9:44 PM—two hours and twenty-four

24

Office of the Medical Examiner
County of Volusia
1360 Indian Lake Road
Daytona Beach, Florida

M.E. Notified Date: _2/26/12_
M.E. Notified Time: _2032_
M.E. Notified By: _FCC_

L.F. Case Number: _2012-J000139_
M.E. Case Number: _12-24-043_
ECS CAD Number: _12-05701994_
Investigator to Scene: ☐ Yes ☐ No

REPORT OF INVESTIGATION BY MEDICAL EXAMINER / INVESTIGATOR

City of Death: _Sanford_
County of Death: _Seminole_

Decedent: _Trayvon_ _____ _Martin_ _Unb 3_
First Name / Middle Name / Last Name / Suffix (Sr., Jr., III)

Address: _____
Number and Street / City, State / Zip Code

Age: _17_ DOB: _04/05/95_ Sex: ☐ Male ☐ Female ☐ Unknown Occupation: _____
Race: ☐ White ☐ Black ☐ Asian ☐ Native American ☐ Hispanic ☐ Other
Marital Status: ☐ Single ☐ Married ☐ Divorced SSN: _____

TYPE OF DEATH (Initial Jurisdiction - Check only one)   _2631 Retreat View Circle Sanford_

☐ Accident - Traffic	☐ Possible Drug Overdose	☐ Violent - Other (found in courtyard)
☐ Accident - Other	☐ Sudden in Apparent Good Health	☐ Non Violent - Suspicious
☐ Homicide	☐ Unattended by Physician	☐ Suspected SIDS / (Or Infant)
☐ Suicide	☐ Homicide/Suicide	☐ Police Custody - Jail/Prison
☐ Natural	☐ Homicide/Suicide (with survivor)	

Notification By: _____ Official Title: _____
Address: _____ Phone: _____
Police Notified: ☐ Yes ☐ No Investigator Contacted: _Semino_ Phone: _407-417-7600_
Address: _____ Jurisdiction: _SPD_

	DATE	TIME (24H)	LOCATION	CITY/COUNTY	TYPE OR PREMISES	BY WHOM
LAST SEEN ALIVE	02/26/12	1915	V	Sanford	Courtyard	resident
INJURY/ ILLNESS		1920	V			
FOUND						
DEATH/PRONOUNCED		1950				SPD

minutes following the death—during which time the victim was lying on the grass exposed to the rain and the elements, apparently only protected by a medical blanket for part of the time.

According to the office records, Investigator Malphurs responded to the scene at 9:44pm and departed only twenty-six minutes later at 10:10pm. This was after the body of Trayvon Martin had been packaged in a blue body bag (tag#VCME000517)) and placed in transport livery van to be taken to the Volusia County Medical Examiner's office where the autopsy would take place.

25

It is quite apparent that no serious independent forensic investigation could have been performed by the Medical Examiner's personnel in the space of twenty-six minutes, which included the time required to package the body and photograph the scene. This is reflected in the investigator's report which turns out to simply be a listing of the "facts" that were provided by law enforcement with no determination of the accuracy or veracity of that information.

NARRATIVE DESCRIPTION OF CIRCUMSTANCES SURROUNDING DEATH:

NEXT OF KIN INFORMATION:

Name:	Relationship:
Address:	Telephone:

Date/Time of ME Arrival: 02/24/12 , 2144   Date/Time ME Departed: 02/24/12 , 2210

While it is the standard procedure in virtually all medical examiner offices throughout the country for the doctor to be at least notified by their investigator in a situation that might possibly turn out to be a homicide, there is no documentation of any contact between Malphurs and the pathologist on call, and clearly no Medical Examiner came to the scene.

As any experienced Medical Examiner can attest, while the forensic investigation is ideally carried out as an objective exercise, there is always the need to eliminate information that may tend to create bias. The analysis needs to be based on 'hard' data, thereby lessening the danger that unsubstantiated information will influence the ultimate final analysis, possibly through erroneous statements and theories, including those made by law enforcement.

In this case, the medical examiner investigator, whose job is to independently analyze the circumstances of a death that comes under the office's jurisdiction, basically took at face value the information that the police provided. She then performed a cursory examination of the body, loaded up the victim and transported him to the morgue—all in the space of 26 minutes.

It was this small amount of information that was provided to the doctor later when the autopsy examination was being done—and apparently very little else. One important, and often critical part of any forensic medico-legal investigation involves ascertaining the condition of the victim's body. This includes the determination of the distribution—or "pattern"—of injuries, the presence or absence of rigor mortis, the temperature of the body, the amount of bleeding or pulmonary edema present, and making an assessment as

26

to how much activity might have been possible on the part of the victim after the wound or wounds were inflicted.

Such determinations can be seriously compromised if any significant time interval occurs between the death and the opportunity for a forensic examiner to be afforded the ability to recognize changes that would not be apparent to law enforcement personnel untrained in these areas. To make and record the observations such as body temperature, presence or absence of rigor mortis, condition and presence of clothing and other items that might be connected to the victim are time sensitive.

For accurate evaluation, ideally there should be minimal if any movement of the victim (other than that reasonably necessary for medical evaluation of the victim's condition), or removal of any items from the deceased.

The medical examiner law in Florida specifically references that issue, stating that the body itself becomes the property of the medical examiner and any alterations from the condition of that body prior to the medical examiner involvement are illegal—possibly a felony depending upon the specific circumstances of that "alteration."

The narrative report from the Medical Examiner investigator indicates that fingerprint identification of the victim was attempted at the scene even though it was raining, and that the prints were sent to the FBI database to determine if the victim had a criminal record with prints on file. It should be noted that fingerprinting is usually performed on the shooter, not the victim.

This is very unusual for any homicide investigation, since it is vital that any trace evidence that might be present on the hands be collected and preserved prior to taking fingerprints.

Printing can be done anytime within a few of days of the death—in order that issues such as the presence or absence of foreign DNA, as well as the presence or absence of gunshot residue in a shooting such as this, can be properly analyzed. The victim's hands were not bagged to protect trace evidence. This is a fundamental procedural error that has never been explained or any effort made to justify the oversight.

One of the most basic standards of good practice in any Medical Examiner's office protocol—and mandated in best practice guidelines for forensic autopsy by the National Association of Medical Examiners (NAME)—is that bags be placed upon a victim's hands prior to moving a body, precisely for the preservation of such potentially critical evidence.

Clearly, manipulating the hands to take fingerprints in a situation where they would get wet and destroy any trace evidence raises the question as to why immediate identification was so critical, since fingerprints can be taken under controlled conditions at the Medical Examiner's office after collecting the trace evidence.

Under Florida law related to the Medical Examiner, a body at the scene of any incident should not be moved or otherwise manipulated by anyone except personnel from the medical examiner's office, after it has been determined that any resuscitative efforts have been discontinued and the victim pronounced dead.

This seems to have been completely ignored by law enforcement at the scene by their actions in obtaining the fingerprints. Why was it so important that it trumped the gathering of trace evidence, including DNA, that might have been critical in either verifying or debunking the story provided to the detectives by the shooter?

The unmistakable conclusion to be drawn here is that the police, encountering a Black male involved in a shooting incident, immediately developed the mindset that the Black male—in this case Trayvon Martin—was the "criminal" in this case. They therefore began to check on a possible criminal record thru the FBI database, which exists primarily to identify criminals.

This is further supported by their approach to the shooter, George Zimmerman, who they didn't immediately arrest, and didn't even begin any prosecution until many weeks following the incident—and only after many protests that gained national media attention.

The Sanford Chief of Police, as seen in the quote above, was already acting as judge and jury making the determination that Zimmerman was innocent of any crime, as it was "self-defense", and they had no intention of pursuing any criminal prosecution.

In reality, one needs to seriously question exactly what information the Chief, as a public official and a sworn police officer, was relying upon to make such a pronouncement, and how he could determine what was the "intent" of the shooter on that evening.

It's clear that the Chief's "intent" was to create a public perception that painted Martin as the aggressor and Zimmerman as the victim, thereby creating a bias that was based upon no verifiable data or evidence.

It is important to note that among those in whom such biases can be created includes the Medical] Examiner, whose job security is to a large degree dependent upon maintaining acordial working relationship with law enforcement.

Many medical examiners have lost their job after crossing swords with the law enforcement agencies in their district, thereby creating an atmosphere that makes speaking out in contradiction to those agencies very risky—and taking the safer route of keeping a "low-profile", much more attractive.

Consequently, even if Dr. Shiping Bao, the Medical Examiner in this case, had been made aware of the potential contradictions between the information being generated from the police department and the forensic "facts", it is unlikely that he would have raised any questions internally and certainly not to the public.

This mindset was carried through to the trial, as will be addressed later, when the supposedly "independent" forensic investigators from the medical examiner's office simply parroted the information that supported the law enforcement theory of what happened on the evening of February 26, 2012.

As any Medical Examiner who has practiced for any length of time and autopsied even a limited number of shooting cases could attest, this is not the approach that would most likely be taken if the shooter was Black and the victim White.

The full autopsy was conducted on February 27, 2012. There does not appear to be any notation or records to establish that there had been any analysis of the clothing worn by the victim, Trayvon Martin.

According to the medical examiner office records, the body was taken to the morgue with all the clothing on or at least with the body according to the property form and was turned over to the Sanford Police Department to begin the Medical Examiner Evaluation. From the autopsy report however, when Dr. Bao first saw the body in the morgue it was unclothed, and there was no description of the clothing included in the records.

According to the medical examiner records, clothing received included a T-shirt, jacket (hoodie), pants, shoes, underwear & watch. The forensic analysis indicated the presence of gunpowder residue on the jacket and undershirt, indicating that the weapon was most likely within several inches away from the victim. Although it is unclear as to whether a more accurate determination by test firing the gun was performed.

One of the very basic abilities to determine the distance of a gunshot firing is to simply fire the same weapon from different distances at white poster board. In this case there was no question as to the weapon and to the ammunition. They had Mr. Zimmerman's firearm and could easily have performed such a test. In this type of test, different pieces of white poster board—like they use in elementary school projects—are mounted at various distances from a fixed firing of the pistol. Generally, one starts at six feet and the results of the "stippling" will be obvious: very faint and widespread. Additional tests are done at five feet, four feet, three feet, two feet, one foot, six inches and contact. In every test the pattern of the stippling will be clear: the closer the range of the shot, the smaller and more condensed the stippling pattern appears.

In this case, had the Medical Examiner's Office and police forensic experts done their job they would have been able to tell conclusively the range of the gunshot within a six-inch variance. They could do the same thing with similar cloth material to the hoodie worn by Martin and then compared the gunshot patterns.

At any rate, the distance of the weapon from the body of the victim was the prime issue that would be addressed during the testimony of the experts during the trial, although there wasn't a real question that the gun was close. The most critical area of consideration should have been the trajectory of the bullet as it relates to the narrative being purported by the shooter.

In addition, fingernail scrapings were taken at autopsy but apparently not analyzed for the presence of DNA or other trace evidence. This valuable evidence almost certainly would have been present if the story given of Martin repeatedly holding Zimmerman's head and pounding it into the cement sidewalk. The analysis of any of this type of transfer evidence including DNA could have either supported or seriously compromised the veracity of the story given by the shooter.

Although the criminalistics report itself could not be obtained because it allegedly no longer exists, depending on the results, it would have certainly been used during the trial.

Parenthetically, it is very difficult to understand how a report, generated electronically, could suddenly "no longer exist."

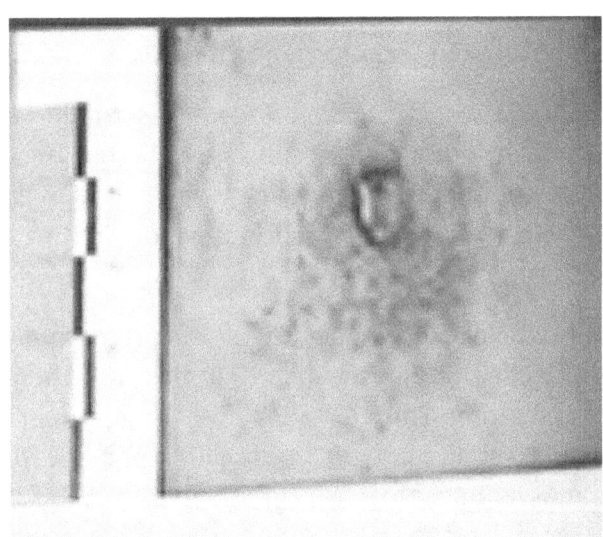

Crime scene photo of wound.

The description of the wound indicates soot at the margins along with an abrasion and a 2" diameter area of stippling. It was determined to be an intermediate-range wound, meaning Martin was 6-30 inches from Zimmerman when he was shot, with no further characterization.

Prior to beginning any dissection, photographs should have been taken of the entire body, including the site of the wound, and x-rays of the chest. In this case, no area of exit of the gunshot was apparent.

Office of the Medical Examiner, Volusia County

Name: UNIDENTIFIED #3.

Age: Race: Black   Sex: Male

Case Number 2012-24043

Date (DR) 7/27/2012 (____)

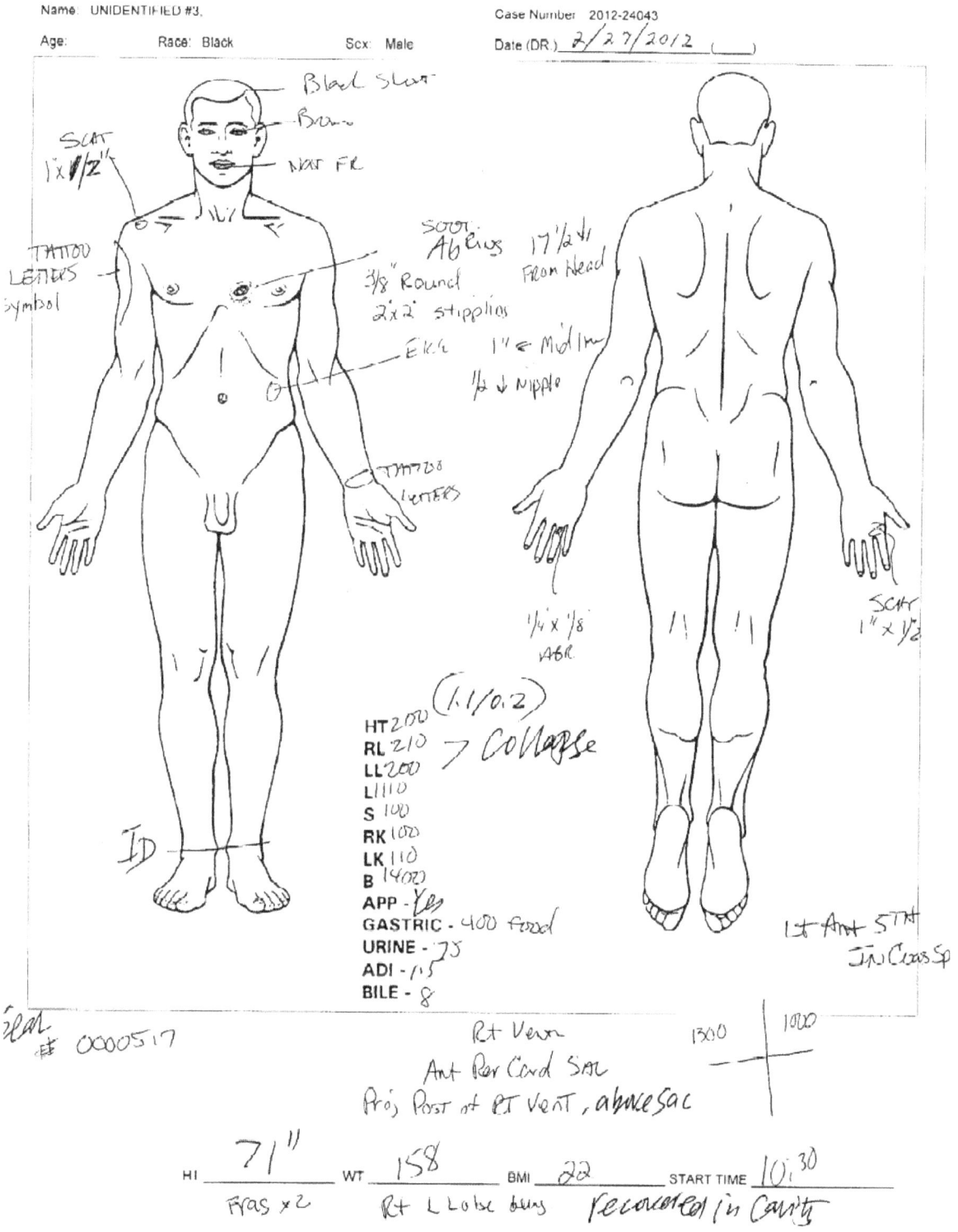

Black Skin
Brow
NAT FR
SCAR 1"x1/2"
TATTOO LETTERS symbol

SOOT Abrus 17 1/2 ↓ From Head
3/8" Round
2"x2" stippling
EKG 1" ← Mid Im
1/2 ↓ Nipple

TATTOO LETTERS

1/4 x 1/8 ABR

SCAR 1" x 1/2

HT 200 (1.1/0.2)
RL 210 → Collapse
LL 200
L 110
S 100
RK 100
LK 110
B 1400
APP - Yes
GASTRIC - 400 food
URINE - 75
ADI - 15
BILE - 8

ID

1st Ant 5TH IN Cross Sp

Slide # 0000517

Rt Vein
Ant Per Cord Sac
Proj Post of RT Vent, above Sac

1300 | 1000

HI 71"   WT 158   BMI 22   START TIME 10:30
Fras x2   Rt L Lobe lung recovered in cavity

31

It is important to accurately determine the location and measure the wounds in any case in which a penetrating injury such as a gunshot wound is present. This is done in order to later determine not only what organs were injured, but also the path of the projectile thru the body. The reference points for these measurements are either from the top of the head or the sole of the foot, and the distance from either side of the midline of the body.

By doing this, a general idea as to the track of the wound can be ascertained. However, the pathologist must recognize that altering the position of either the victim or the shooter may cause the tracks to be different from when the body is examined lying in the so-called anatomic position — on his or her back, hands to the side, and legs straight.

This wound was located 17 ½ inches from the top of the head, and 1 inch to the left of the midline, and ½ inch below the nipple (line) in the anterior chest, left of the left margin of the sternum.

The wound was roughly circular, measuring 0.8 cm (about 3/8 inch) in diameter with an area of abrasion, or scraping of the skin, located circumferentially around the central wound hole, indicative of an entry gunshot wound.

As a bullet is entering the skin, the front of the projectile pushes a small circle of skin inwardly, in addition to the actual hole, creating this characteristic pattern, thus allowing the pathologist to determine that this was a wound of entry.

A wound of exit in contrast, simply creates a tear in the skin with no abrasion ring since the bullet is pushing the skin from the inside outwardly and there is no scraping.

Also, burned and unburned powder is expelled from the muzzle of a firearm when fired and may be helpful in determining the range of fire since the unburned soot travels about 6-8 inches in air, and the burned powder can travel up to 24 inches.

When burning powder strikes the skin, small punctate areas of burning are produced creating a phenomenon known as "stippling." Analysis of this stippling pattern can help in determining the distance between the firearm and the victim.

Clothing, as well as any object between the shooter and the victim, can block gunpowder elements from reaching the skin, making it essential to examine clothing to determine the range of fire.

Dr. Bao describes in the autopsy report the organs involved by the wound track, indicating a path of "front-to-back" that would later be described as "straight back" in courtroom testimony.

MEDICAL EXAMINER REPORT
REPORT OF AUTOPSY

EVIDENCE OF INJURY

Penetrating Gunshot Wound of the Chest:

The entrance wound is located on the left chest, 17½ inches below the top of the head, 1 inch to the left of the anterior midline, and ½ inch below the nipple. It consists of a ⅜ inch diameter round entrance defect with soot, ring abrasion, and a 2 x 2 inch area of stippling. This wound is consistent with a wound of entrance of intermediate range.

Further examination demonstrates that the wound track passes directly from front to back and enters the pleural cavity with perforations of the left anterior fifth intercostal space, pericardial sac, right ventricle of the heart, and the right lower lobe of the lung. There is no wound of exit.

Three fragments of projectile are recovered. The lead core is recovered in the pericardial sac behind the right ventricle. Two fragments of the jacket are recovered in the right pleural cavity behind the right lower lobe of the lung.

The injuries associated with the wound: The entrance wound; perforations of left anterior fifth intercostal space, pericardial sac, right ventricle of the heart, right lower lobe of the lung with approximately 1300 milliliters of blood in the right pleural cavity and 1000 in the left pleural cavity; the collapse of both lungs.

Other injuries: There is a ¼ x ⅛ inch small abrasion on the left fourth finger.

In any anatomic reconstruction of the injury and shown in a reconstruction diagram drawn for the purpose of demonstration and shown below, it was clear that since the right ventricle (RV) and right lung (RL) are both to the right of the documented point of entry into the left side of the chest, (with perforations of the left anterior fifth intercostal space), directionality was left to right and not "directly backward." The following illustrations below provide a graphic depiction of the trajectory of the bullet's pathway as it enters the victim's chest.

Furthermore, one relatively large fragment of the bullet—the lead core—was recovered in the pericardial sac (the sac surrounding the heart) behind the right ventricle, and two fragments of the jacket found in the right pleural cavity, behind the lower lobe of the right lung. (See illustration on the next page.)

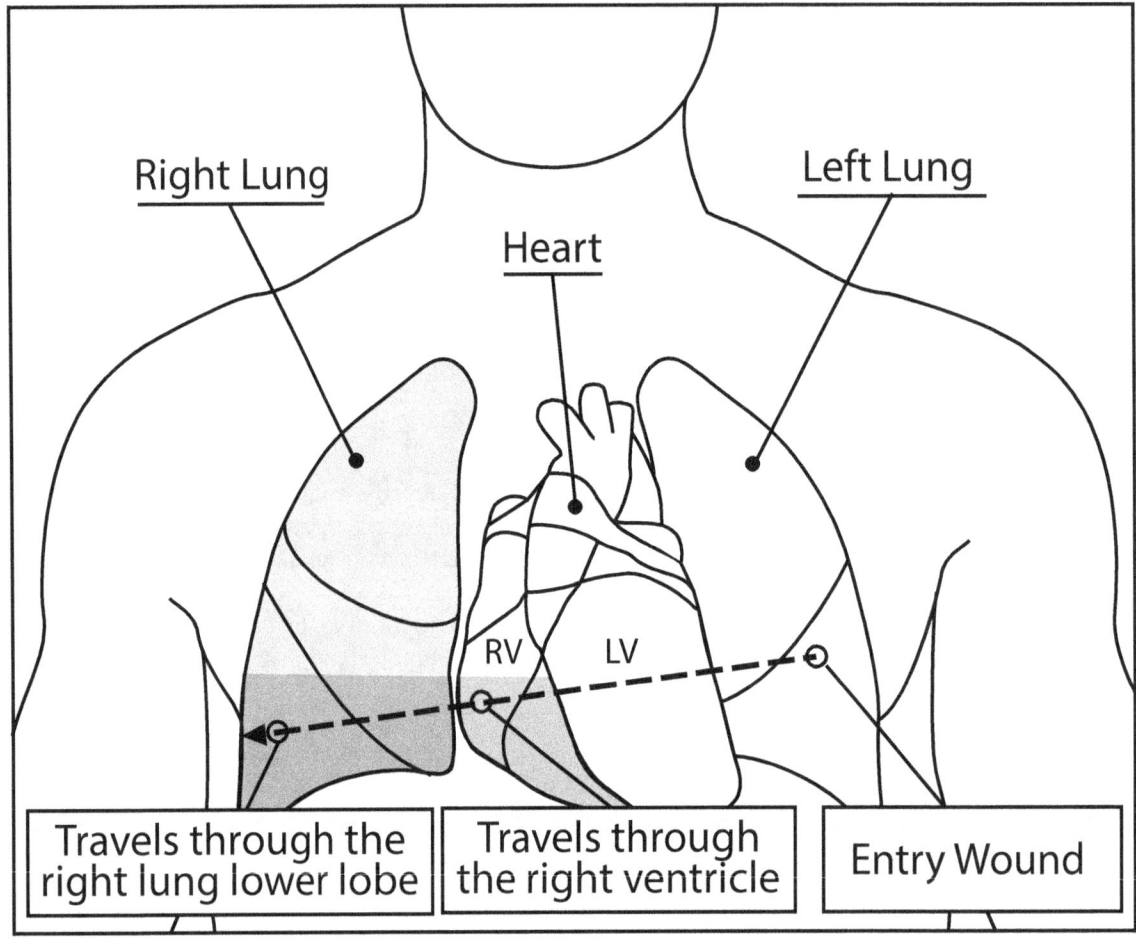

Right Lung

Left Lung

Heart

RV   LV

Travels through the right lung lower lobe | Travels through the right ventricle | Entry Wound

The pathologist apparently failed to recognize this, and it would prove to be a critically important issue in the future of this case, since reconstruction of the positions of victim and shooter completely contradicts the story given police by the shooter. A contradiction that was not apparently recognized, or if recognized certainly not resolved at any point in the investigation or subsequent prosecution of the case.

The complete dissection of the remaining organs revealed no underlying disease processes, and the death was considered to be a single gunshot wound to the chest.

Importantly, it was also noted that there were no other areas of trauma to the body, including examination of the hands and forearms for evidence of abrasion or contusion that might indicate that the victim had been in an altercation. There were also no offensive or defensive wounds identified anywhere on Trayvon Martin's body.

On the left hand there were some old abrasions, but no scrapes or apparent indications of any recent injury to any degree on any of the knuckles of the victim. There was no swelling to any of the joints in either hand which could be indicative of punches thrown against a hard object, like the head of another person. There were no cracks, breaks or chips or any apparent injuries of any type to any of the fingernails.

Further examination revealed total absence of any kind of irritation, bruising, scrapes or any trauma to either of the knees, which would indicate a person kneeling over an object of battle.

There were no bruises on either of the forearms inside or out. In other words, there was not a single indication by close examination in the morgue of any corroborating evidence that the victim had been in a fight with another individual.

After the actual dissection, the physical part of the autopsy was completed. Standard procedure dictates that the medical examiner would examine all the data available including that which had been collected at the autopsy, as well as information about the incident, and draw a conclusion from that information in determining the Cause and Manner of Death.

A complete autopsy includes observing the body and all the various organs with the naked eye to evaluate the presence or absence of any injuries, the distribution or pattern of those injuries identified, determining what if any underlying natural disease processes may be present – and possibly having contributed to the death. In addition to this, the Medical Examiner examines tissue samples under the microscope and performs laboratory analysis of fluids and tissues to detect the presence of drugs or other toxic substances.

Consequently, the final determination regarding the causation of death isn't made until all the data has been analyzed and the entire case reviewed – a process that may take several weeks or more depending upon the complexity of the case.

Unfortunately, in many instances, the findings from the initial autopsy become public and are henceforth treated as the final diagnosis. This particularly occurs in situations where individuals from outside the medical examiner's office may be present, including members of law enforcement in situations of suspected Homicide.

This can become particularly problematic when the results from the additional tests, or more detailed analysis of the initial findings, substantially affect the ultimate diagnosis and interpretation of the autopsy. Often, especially in high-profile cases, preliminary details have been widely circulated in the public and the press, making it very difficult politically for a pathologist to back-track and correct the record. If they do, they run the risk of suffering damage to their professional reputation, and quite likely, their job.

Chapter Three

THE LEGAL GAMES BEGIN

As was alluded to earlier, the shooter was not "officially" arrested. This was a highly unusual, if not entirely improbable circumstance. Given the undisputed facts of what the scene revealed, the responding police apparently made no formal declarations of intent to arrest and seize Mr. Zimmerman.

Ordinary exposure to police conduct and confrontations of suspects make an evaluation of this situation highly questionable. It is undisputed that there was only one "suspect" in the area of the crime scene: Mr. Zimmerman. There had been one shot fired, that by Zimmerman with his gun. There was one victim, young Trayvon, who was lying there with a hole in his chest.

One would ordinarily expect that the responding police would have immediately drawn their weapons and ordered the suspect to put his hands behind his head and kneel on the ground.

Whether in the exact confrontation or not, it is clear that one would ordinarily expect a responding police officer to take control and order the suspect down.

Mr. Zimmerman, instead of having been ordered to the ground and disarmed at gunpoint, was allowed to just simply stand there, and state his apparent "defense." There was no doubt of the facts as simple as they were: one suspect, one victim, one shot.

Zimmerman was not in any uniform or displaying any type of hat, clothing, official indication, words of any description, to cause anyone coming upon him to realize he was some form of police officer.

Apparently, based on some immediate declarations, the shooter conveyed to responding officers that he was a "watch commander", therefore, some sort of official person. This appears to have caused him to be considered within the "police-buddy cop category." There does not appear to be any doubt that Zimmerman was given preferential treatment by the responding officers, and later by the Prosecution and State Attorney's Office.

A review of the history of the arrest procedures in this case raises significant questions. If the responding police officers had handled this case from the beginning as is normally expected, the later nationwide outrage would have been avoided. The police officers arriving at the scene would have avoided all their now questionable behavior by just following normal protocol.

Mr. Zimmerman should have been booked in the standard ordinary process. His lawyer then would have immediately been able to file a Motion or simply appear at the next morning's court, "first appearances", and orally seek the liberal conditions of release for Mr. Zimmerman. Routinely, the Court would either order a bail bond to be posted or establish other conditions.

The Court could just as easily have ordered Zimmerman, who was a long term resident, to be released on his recognizance pending notification of other proceedings.

The Prosecution would then have done its investigation, or at least preliminary levels of investigation, and determined what formal charges to be filed against Mr. Zimmerman, if any. Since there was not even a "formal arrest" and complete freedom conditions established for the suspect, none of that occurred.

He was simply allowed to go home, carry on with his ordinary life, and wait to see if the Prosecution ever did anything. Instead, as we saw, there was a huge national outcry complaining of the unusually favorable treatment for Mr. Zimmerman.

As a matter of law, there are no "magic words" that are required to be iterated by the police or any other official to constitute an "arrest." All that is required to establish that an arrest is taking place is "to deprive a person of his liberty by legal authority or to restrain that individual, however slight, so that their liberty is restricted as to their ability to come and go."

In this case no such declaration was made. All that can be established based on the police reports and later statements by Mr. Zimmerman is that he was "escorted" to the police department. He was not read his rights as one might get used to seeing on television shows. There were no formal "declarations." Mr. Zimmerman was voluntarily handcuffed when in the police department.

According to what is obvious from the video, Mr. Zimmerman was under the control of police officers, he was handcuffed, and he was in the police department. He was at some point thereafter questioned minimally about the event. He was not required to post any kind of bond, agree to any more formal restraints, and allowed to go on about his business and go home.

Under the undisputed reports as well as admissions from Mr. Zimmerman, it is hard to imagine that he was not "formally" arrested at the scene and at least in some fashion accused of some crime. In any normal circumstance with reasonable expectations, he would have been specifically told he was "under arrest", taken to the jail, mugshots taken, booked, printed, and advised as to the nature of the charge against him. In the most liberal of circumstances, he could have simply been given a notice to appear and be required to do so before a Court immediately (within one or two days). This was not done.

As we know, this failure to "arrest" and "formally charge" created a nationwide outcry concerning the unusually favorable, if not prejudicial, position by the police department. The result was the creation of a political movement known as Black Lives Matter (#blacklivesmatter), as a direct response to the acquittal of Mr. Zimmerman in this case and has been carried out by the Black Lives Matter nationwide, through today, more than a decade later.

Chapter Four

DECLINING PROSECUTION: SEMINOLE COUNTY STATE ATTORNEY

The clear facts were that Zimmerman began an active stalking pursuit of the victim and precipitated the sequence of events that led to the shooting,

In a "stand your ground" State such as Florida, Trayvon, a teenage boy, would have reason to fear harm from an unknown adult who was stalking him around the complex where he was staying with his father.

The immediate focus however appears to have been to consider Zimmerman more in the light of a victim's role who was attacked by this Black teenager wearing a hoodie, in a scenario wherein the shooter was the victim.

The subsequent adoption of this theory is best portrayed in the actions of the police, the State Attorney's Office, the press and to some extent by the Medical Examiner.

Examination of the Medical Examiner office records show no documentation of any meetings with the Law Enforcement Agency (LEA) or State Attorney's Office (SAO) in the days following the shooting. There also wasn't any fact checking that took place between the detectives involved in the reconstruction of the events and the pathologist who performed the autopsy, to verify that the two were consistent and in agreement.

This obviously would be important so that any inconsistencies—such as the directionality of the bullet trajectory through Martin's body—could be discovered and subsequently addressed.

Instead, the accuracy of the reconstruction video as created the day following the incident by the police and Zimmerman was accepted at face value and presented as factual throughout the course of the prosecution's investigation and subsequently to the jury at the trial.

When evidence is presented to a jury of lay persons, particularly when introduced by the Prosecution, there is a strong presumption that the evidence is reliable, and the information is accurate—since in most instances there is nothing in the presentation that would suggest otherwise.

In almost all circumstances, that presumption is justified, since an adequately investigated criminal case would have all information completely vetted and any inconsistencies resolved in advance of that case even being charged, let alone being presented to a jury at trial.

That clearly does not appear to be what happened in the shooting death of Trayvon Martin. As regards the actual autopsy performed on the morning after the shooting, it is particularly noteworthy that under the section headed "Officials Present at Autopsy", is the entry "None", indicating that no law enforcement personnel, including the detectives allegedly involved in the investigation were there.

Name   Martin, Trayvon   ME #   12-24-043

MEDICAL EXAMINER REPORT
REPORT OF AUTOPSY

OFFICIALS PRESENT AT EXAMINATION

None.

EXTERNAL EXAMINATION

The body is secured in a blue body bag with Medical Examiner seal #0000517.

The body is viewed unclothed. The body is that of a normally developed, black male appearing the stated age of 17 years with a body length of 71 inches and body weight of 158 pounds. The body presents a medium build with average nutrition, normal hydration and good preservation. Rigor mortis is complete, and lividity is well developed and fixed on the posterior surfaces of the body. The body is cold to touch post refrigeration. Short black hair covers the scalp. The face is unremarkable. There is average body hair of adult-male-pattern distribution. The eyes are closed and have clear bulbar and palpebral conjunctivae. The irides are brown with white sclerae. There are no cataracts or arcus present. The pupils are equal at 5 millimeters. The orbits appear normal. The nasal cavities are unremarkable with an intact septum. The oral cavity presents natural teeth with fair oral hygiene. The ears are unremarkable with no hemorrhage in the external auditory canals. The neck is rigid due to postmortem changes, and there are no palpable masses. The chest is symmetrical. The abdomen is scaphoid.

The upper and lower extremities are equal and symmetrical and present cyanotic nail beds without clubbing or edema. There are no fractures, deformities or amputations present. The external genitalia present descended testicles and an unremarkable penis. The back reveals dependent lividity with contact pallor. The buttocks are atraumatic, and the anus is intact. The integument is of normal color.

OTHER IDENTIFYING FEATURES

There are identification bands on the ankles.

SCARS
- 1 x ½ inch scar - right shoulder
- 1 x ½ inch scar - right hand

TATTOOS
- Symbol with letters - right arm
- Letters - left wrist

There are no other significant identifying features.

It is the experience of any forensic pathologist who has practiced for any length of time in a Medical Examiner or Coroner's office, that one of the major occupational hazards in the performance of an objective, scientific medico-legal autopsy is the introduction of potential biases. These potential biases are a result of external inputs of biased information or data from sources that might serve to influence the direction taken by the doctor, either early in the process or during the actual autopsy dissection.

Although every effort may be made to ensure every autopsy is as close to an unbiased scientific evaluation as possible, it often takes a conscious effort to tune-out such outside influences that might affect the entire process. Especially when most often those influences come directly from the law enforcement officers involved in the investigation. It was an almost universal, and often not welcomed practice on the part of law enforcement for the detectives investigating a homicide to be present at the actual autopsy.

Their inputs to the pathologist regarding their theory of what events had taken place leading up to the death of the person involved can be highly influential. This process often leads the pathologist to make certain assumptions that could seriously affect his or her ability to maintain the objectivity required to make a determination based upon the factual forensic findings.

Too often the initial theories developed by law enforcement turn out to be totally incorrect and could lead the pathologist to an erroneous conclusion had that information been relied upon in coming to a conclusion regarding the death.

Certain autopsy procedures might be deemed not necessary by the pathologist performing an autopsy if the circumstances surrounding the death suggested those procedures were irrelevant in a particular circumstance.

Many Medical Examiner offices discourage outside agencies, particularly law enforcement, from attending the actual autopsy to allow the pathologist to look at the actual hard data prior to learning what the police thought happened and what were thought to be the circumstances surrounding the death.

As it turned out when the autopsy on Trayvon Martin was performed on the morning following the shooting, Dr. Bao didn't need to worry about any of these potential problems. None of the detectives investigating the case— or for that matter, anyone from either law enforcement or the State Attorney's office— appeared to be interested enough to even show up at the autopsy. This rather strange behavior for a potential Homicide case would only portend the series of inexplicable events that were to follow.

Autopsies are large surgical procedures during which all parts of the body are examined, multiple tissue and body fluid samples gathered for analysis, both under the microscope and in the clinical laboratory. Consequently, they involve several stages, requiring several weeks or more to arrive at a finished or final report of the findings and conclusions.

The first part of any autopsy involves a significant number of individual procedures that include examining the deceased externally then making note of clothing, body temperature and absence of rigor mortis. Any obvious external injuries such as bruises, cuts, stab wounds and gunshot wounds are documented. As well as collecting any trace evidence that may prove important in any ensuing investigation of the death.

Following the external examination, the head, chest, and abdominal cavities are accessed through large surgical incisions—commonly referred to as the "Y-shaped incision"—after which the skullcap and chest plate are removed, allowing the organs to be examined in place, as well as individually removed for a more detailed evaluation.

The organs are then weighed individually to determine if they are of normal size and weight and then dissected—examining their blood and nerve supplies, looking for areas of inflammation, recent injury, or scarring that might indicate old injury that could be related in some way to the death of the patient.

Additionally, small biopsies of each organ are taken and processed for later examination under the microscope, cultures taken for microbiological cultures, and samples of blood and other fluids are collected for later analysis.

In many instances, x-ray and other radiological images are made of various areas of the body to discover and document fractures and the presence of foreign bodies, such as projectiles.

The data from all these various studies will ultimately be considered in the formulation of the diagnosis determining the cause of death and the manner whether natural, homicide, suicide or accidental in nature.

According to the autopsy report from the pathologist, Dr. Shiping Bao, the body of Trayvon Martin is described as unclothed, indicating that he was not able to view the deceased prior to removal of his clothing.

Although it is often critical—and certainly considered best-practice—for purposes of orientation of any injuries, that the person performing the autopsy have access to the body prior to any items, including clothing, being altered, or removed.

This clearly did not happen in the case of Trayvon Martin since he already had all clothing removed prior to the pathologist viewing the body according to his own report. This is a clear and very significant departure from acceptable practices, particularly in situations involving a potential homicide.

According to the records, the pathologist states under the External Examination: "The body is secured in a blue body bag with Medical Examiner seal 0000517", followed by "The body is viewed unclothed", indicating that the clothing must have been removed prior to the victim being placed in the body bag and the bag sealed until opened by the pathologist.

Multiple unfulfilled requests were made to the Medical Examiner's office for photos of the scene and autopsy. The autopsy photos are protected under Florida law and require the permission of the victim's family to be released. This was due to the so-called "Earnhardt Law", enacted after the public backlash when the pathologist performing the autopsy photos of race car driver Dale Earnhardt, killed during the Daytona 500 stock-car race posted them on the internet.

The race-car community had placed enough pressure on the Legislature to pass a law restricting access to medical examiner autopsy photos by anyone besides law enforcement and State prosecutors. The law severely restricts the ability for outsiders to investigate any case in the future that might, depending upon the circumstances, require further scrutiny apart from information released to the public.

Review of the records further indicates that the clothing, at least in part, was ultimately released by the medical examiner's office to the Sanford Police Department, but there is no documentation that any trace evidence from the clothing was even collected let alone analyzed.

Fingernail clippings, hair and blood samples, blood for DNA and toxicology were taken from Martin's body as is standard procedure.

According to the records, toxicology testing was done on the blood, but no analysis of the clothing was done, and there was no testing of the other items, including the finger-nails, which could have potentially confirmed contact between he and Zimmerman had DNA testing been performed.

As referenced earlier, the narrative report of the medical examiner investigator Mal-phurs indicates that fingerprint identification was attempted by the police at the scene, apparently even though it was raining, which is very unusual since it is often critical that the hands be placed in paper bags to protect from the potential loss of valuable trace evidence.

It is particularly unusual to take prints immediately from a victim of homicide for that very reason. The manipulation of Trayvon Martin's hands during the fingerprinting process essentially contaminated his hands and destroyed any evidence that may have been there, such as transfer DNA that might clarify how much interaction there actually had been between the two individuals.

Because of the allegation that Martin repeatedly banged Zimmerman's head against the sidewalk and caused lacerations of the scalp with bleeding, the presence or absence of transfer blood on Martin's hands would have been much more important than the totally unnecessary rapid identification of the victim at the scene.

No apparent attempt was made to find out the identity of this then unidentified Black male. His father had been calling police reporting a missing person following the shooting, when finally, the police were able to make the connection and notify Trayvon's father who made a photographic identification on 02/28/1012, a full two days after the shooting.

The autopsy report was completed and finalized on 03/15/2012, a little more than two weeks after the death of Trayvon Martin, representing a very rapid turnaround time since in most Medical Examiner's offices, the finalization may take three to four months, if not longer.

Up until that point, according to office records, there was no peer review by a second pathologist or supervisor in the office prior to making a final determination. Only proof-reading of the autopsy draft was performed and then the report was signed out as finalized.

Surprisingly there were no recorded contacts with any members of the LEA or SAO prior to the issuance of the report.

In fact, there was no record of any contact with any members of the State Attorney or Law Enforcement until the depositions were taken eight months later of Investigator Malphrus and Dr. Bao. Apparently, Bao had his only recorded meeting with SAO a few days before his testimony and they only discussed the photos that the state planned to show. Nothing else regarding the case was discussed.

In virtually every situation involving a Homicide, contact between the law enforcement agencies and the Medical Examiner occurs from the very first moments of the incident. Often even becoming intrusive to the point of raising the possibility of introducing bias to the doctor's opinions while the medical evaluations are being done.

The lack of involvement raises a serious question as to whether the State had already decided not to pursue this shooting as a murder or write it off as a justifiable homicide.

The reports of the Medical Examiner as to what he did or did not do, provide no answers. The police department simply took Mr. Zimmerman's word as if it were the truth, and therefore could just overlook the fact that this unarmed victim was lying on the ground with a bullet hole through his chest.

The chief of police exclaimed that there was no arrest because he felt like they had no "probable cause" to make an arrest. There were no eyewitnesses to support the claim. All that was undisputed is that there was a dead body, and he was unarmed.

If there was no probable cause to arrest in this case, then that rationalization would eliminate probably nearly 90% of the homicides in history. The term "probable cause" is one that is often misused by non-lawyers, politicians, and people with relevant motives.

What it really means, as defined in the law historically, is that an apparent state of facts is found to exist that upon reasonable inquiry would give a sound, prudent person belief that a crime had been committed. Here, the undisputed facts are fairly simple: there was a dead victim who was unarmed and a perpetrator who acknowledged the shooting but tried to claim that he acted in self-defense.

Chapter Five

REENACTMENT OF THE SHOOTING

The very next day following the incident, the shooter was afforded the opportunity to perform a video-taped reenactment of the incident showing the pathway the shooter allegedly took through the apartment complex where he had encountered Trayvon, how he was subsequently punched in the nose, wrestled to the ground, and while on the ground had his head slammed repeatedly into the cement sidewalk.

At some point while Trayvon, who was then allegedly on top, reached across with his right hand in an attempt to grab Zimmerman's gun, which was located on or near the latter's right hip. Zimmerman then pulled out the weapon and fired a single shot.

According to statements made by Zimmerman to the police, Martin then fell backwards onto the ground—saying something to the effect of "you got me!"

Media interviews later with Zimmerman's father quoted him saying that Martin said "You die today"—information he'd apparently received from his son at some point.

None of this self-serving production was verified in anyway by objective evidence and entirely premised on the assumption that Zimmerman was telling the truth. There were virtually no references to any type of scene investigation by law enforcement other than to simply document the position of the body.

The first most obvious problem with this theory is that from the pictures of Martin on the ground, he appears to be in a completely grassed area, with no sidewalk nearby. Zimmerman's defense attorneys made it quite an issue that Trayvon would have lived no more than one to three minutes following the gunshot wound that involved his heart—meaning that he would have most likely died at the location he was shot.

The severity of the injuries to the heart and both lungs documented at autopsy would certainly indicate that there was little, if any, purposeful activity after the injury, and in view of the shooter's claim that his head was being pounded into the cement sidewalk, the body should have been on or at least in the near proximity of a cement sidewalk.

In the photo on the next page the body has been rolled over presumably by first responders attempting to assess the condition of the victim and initiate CPR.

There was no evidentiary basis for law enforcement to even entertain the possibility that this video demonstration should be given any credibility, but somehow it was never challenged and even ended up being presented by the State Prosecutors at trial.

At the time of the video recording, there is no evidence of any involvement on the part of Dr. Bao or anyone from the Medical Examiner's office in verification of such things as the relative position of shooter and victim or range of fire as determined by the characteristics of the wound. These details are key to understanding what happened and confirmed to reveal any potential inconsistencies between the shooter's story and the forensic evidence.

50

A group of detectives, with no apparent guidance from any medical personnel possessing the capability to relate the actual factual data to the reenactment being undertaken, staged the event based solely upon the direction of the shooter who had perpetrated the shooting.

We were unable to obtain any records from the police pertaining to how this event was allowed to take place. There is no record of who gave the directives to make the video or why it was created. It is very unlikely that formal records were not made of who authorized this event. Any evidence as to how far up the chain of command the decision was made has apparently been destroyed or at least not made accessible to the public.

This is an apparent problem with Florida's so-called open records policy, the "Sunshine Law" which allegedly gives the public access to governmental records in order to maintain transparency.

Based upon existing procedures it is a legitimate question as to how this video, with its total lack of any scientifically verifiable facts, eventually made it all the way to the trial to become a centerpiece of the prosecution's case.

In the description of the injuries provided by the pathologist from the autopsy, the bullet entered the anterior chest wall 1" to the left of the midline, perforating the 5th intercostal space, and then passing through the pericardial sac surrounding the heart, perforating the right ventricle of the heart and then striking the lower lobe of the right lung.

51

Both lungs are described as collapsed or atelectatic, indicating that both pleural cavities were involved. In order for this bilateral involvement to occur, anatomically the bullet would necessarily have traveled in a left-to-right direction, and not directly backwards as Dr. Bao describes both in his autopsy report and later in testimony at trial.

This clear discrepancy was apparently neither recognized nor addressed by anyone involved except possibly the defense expert pathologist, Dr. Vincent DiMaio, a renowned expert in gunshot wounds during his trial testimony, who conveniently overlooked the issue—and for good reason.

The major issue was not that the gun was discharged at close range, since there is stippling pattern eccentric with angulation downward indicating the gun was at a point above the entry wound with the burning gunpowder spraying out resulting with a wider pattern along the direction of the projectile.

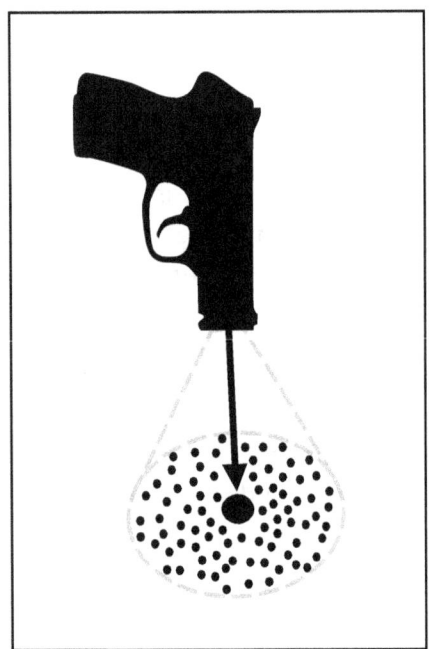

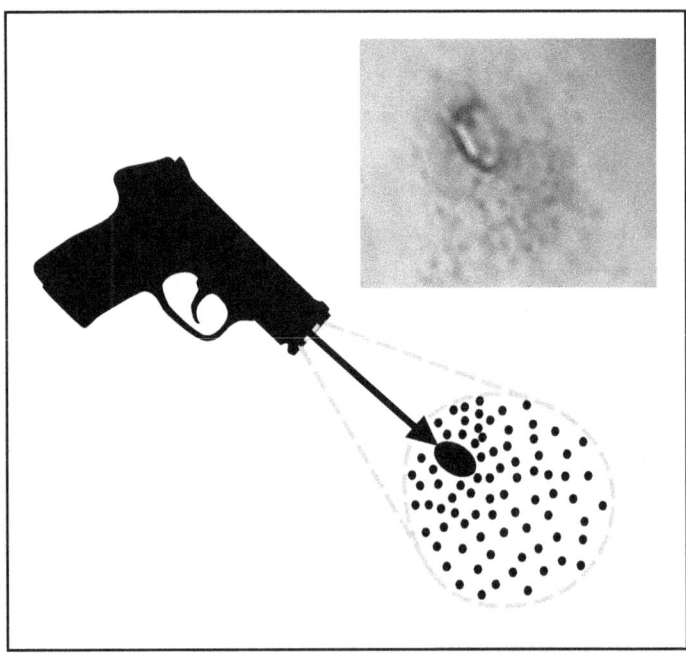

Gunpowder scatter pattern if the gun was shot perpendicular to the body

Gunpowder scatter pattern if the gun was shot at an angle to the body, and (the actual photo of the wound (inset) showing the scatter.

The distribution of the burned gunpowder (referred to as stippling) will vary considerably depending upon the angulation of the gun barrel relative to the skin surface of the victim as illustrated in the above diagram.

Analysis of the gunshot trajectory from the description provided in the autopsy report confirms the left-to-right direction and points out an apparently completely overlooked factor that is critical to the analysis of the events surrounding the shooting.

Name   Martin, Trayvon   ME #   12-24-043

MEDICAL EXAMINER REPORT
REPORT OF AUTOPSY

EVIDENCE OF INJURY

Penetrating Gunshot Wound of the Chest:

The entrance wound is located on the left chest, $17\frac{1}{2}$ inches below the top of the head, 1 inch to the left of the anterior midline, and $\frac{1}{2}$ inch below the nipple. It consists of a $\frac{3}{8}$ inch diameter round entrance defect with soot, ring abrasion, and a 2 x 2 inch area of stippling. This wound is consistent with a wound of entrance of intermediate range.

Further examination demonstrates that the wound track passes directly from front to back and enters the pleural cavity with perforations of the left anterior fifth intercostal space, pericardial sac, right ventricle of the heart, and the right lower lobe of the lung. There is no wound of exit.

Three fragments of projectile are recovered. The lead core is recovered in the pericardial sac behind the right ventricle. Two fragments of the jacket are recovered in the right pleural cavity behind the right lower lobe of the lung.

The injuries associated with the wound: The entrance wound; perforations of left anterior fifth intercostal space, pericardial sac, right ventricle of the heart, right lower lobe of the lung with approximately 1300 milliliters of blood in the right pleural cavity and 1000 in the left pleural cavity; the collapse of both lungs.

Other injuries: There is a $\frac{1}{4}$ x $\frac{1}{8}$ inch small abrasion on the left fourth finger.

EVIDENCE OF RECENT MEDICAL TREATMENT

There is a cardiac monitor pad on the left flank.

EVIDENCE OF ORGAN AND/OR TISSUE DONATION

None.

INTERNAL EXAMINATION: The following excludes any previously described injuries.

BODY CAVITIES

The peritoneum is congested, smooth, glistening and essentially dry; devoid of adhesions or effusion. There is no scoliosis, kyphosis or lordosis present. The left and right diaphragms are in their normal location and appear grossly unremarkable.

In the video re-enactment, Mr. Zimmerman can be observed demonstrating their relative positions with himself on his back on the ground and Trayvon Martin on top. He further clearly demonstrates that Martin reached across his body with his right hand attempting to presumably grab the weapon that Zimmerman had apparently holstered on his right side.

That sequence of events was created on video by Mr. Zimmerman himself and recorded contemporaneously by the detectives from the Sanford Police Department—later to be presented by the State Prosecutor under color of fact.

When an individual reaches across his or her chest with either arm, the entire thoracic cavity is rotated either clockwise or counterclockwise depending upon which arm is involved.

The rotation of the thorax described in the video re-enactment would have resulted in the left side of the chest being elevated upwards and, in this position, a bullet entering the left side of the chest would involve the anterior portion of the left ventricle of the heart and the left lung.

There would be no left to right trajectory if the events depicted in the video were correct. With the chest in that position the path wouldn't even be straight back.

The actual trajectory would be from right to left striking the left lung, ending up in the posterior chest wall on the left, not the right side.

The diagram below depicts the actual path of the bullet as it was documented at the autopsy description, with injury to the left rib cage, right ventricle of the heart and right lung.

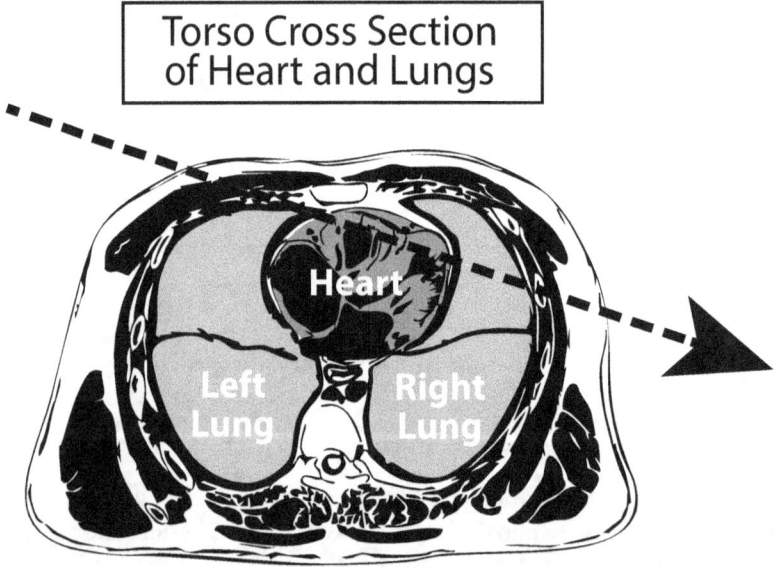

Torso Cross Section of Heart and Lungs

If a person begins to turn to their left, the rotation of the chest and internal organs creates a different trajectory (the trajectory marker remaining stationary, and the diagram of the chest being rotated) creating injury to the left ventricle of the heart, the right atrium of the heart, and posterior part of the right lung as pictured below.

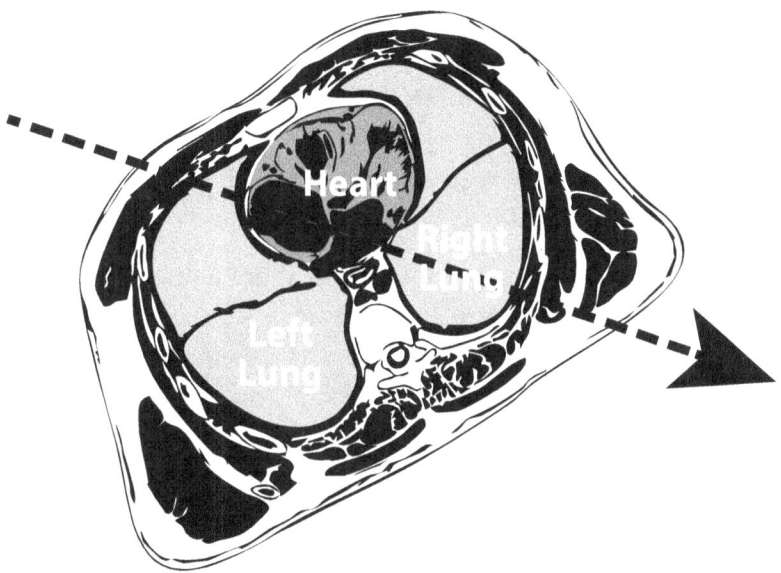

Further leftwards rotation (again keeping the trajectory marker stationary and rotating the diagram) as would be the case if Trayvon had been on top and reaching across with his right hand attempting to reach the gun on Zimmerman's right hip, there would be a completely different trajectory from what was actually found at autopsy. The projectile would either miss or graze the left ventricle and continue into the left lung.

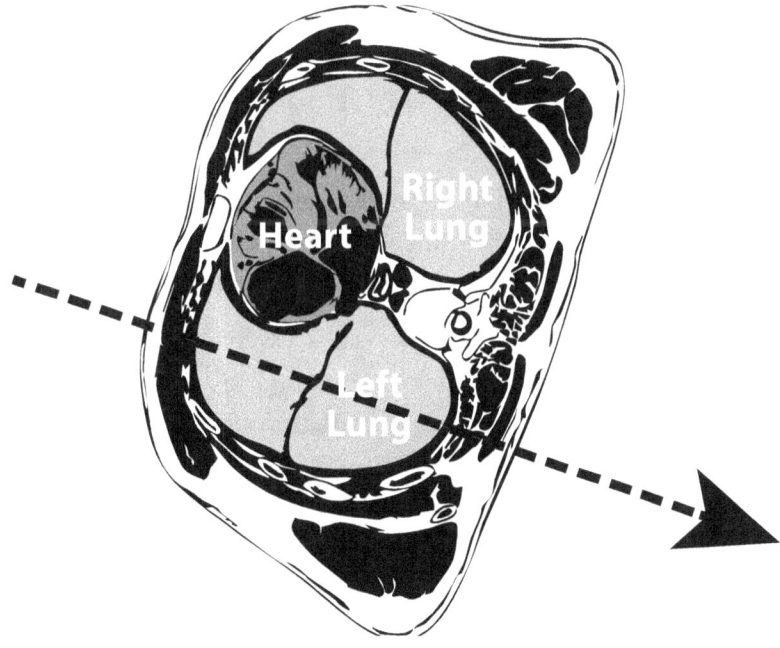

The bullet would have traveled right-to-left, not left-to-right— the trajectory proven at the autopsy.

That clearly refutes through scientific evidence, the account given by the shooter in the self-styled video re-enactment.

Additionally, it must be noted that the entrance wound on the chest is at the level of the base of the heart, the right and left atria, and the beginning or root of the aorta, and the upper lobes of both the right and left lungs. In order for the projectile to end up perforating the lower lobe of the right lung (or either lung for that matter) there must be a significant degree of downward direction as well.

This downward trajectory matches perfectly with the stippling pattern which shows a pattern, as described above, consistent with the barrel of the gun at an angle relative to the skin surface. The gun was directed from above the entry wound hole, with only a small amount of stippling on the upper margin, where the skin is protected by the barrel itself, and spraying out in the direction of fire.

In other words, the shooter was above the victim, possibly standing while Trayvon was partly down on the ground, when the shot was fired. He was not on top of Zimmerman reaching across his body attempting to take the weapon from the holster on the right hip.

Had the law enforcement personnel had any contact at all with the Medical Examiner prior to creating and accepting this account, it would have become apparent that there were some serious inconsistencies. These inconsistencies should have been explored and resolved, prior to accepting it as factual to the point of the Prosecution's allowing its presentation at the trial.

Because it was presented by the State and obviously not challenged by the Defense counsel, there was no possible way the jurors could be expected to realize that this evidence was completely false. A fact that further raises serious questions as to the actual motives of the State in this situation.

There were some old abrasions on the left hand, but no scrapes or apparent indications of any recent injury to any degree on any of the knuckles of either hand of Trayvon. There was no swelling to any of the joints in either hand which could be indicative of punches thrown against the head of another person.

There were no cracks, breaks or chips or any apparent injuries of any type to any of the fingernails. Although samples were taken of the fingernails for forensic analysis potentially looking for DNA – fingernail scrapings – those were apparently never analyzed as there were no reports of any results, and the issue was never raised by anyone at trial.

Further examination as depicted in the Medical Examiners body diagram reveals the total absence of any kind of irritation, bruising, scrapes or any trauma to either of Trayvon's

Office of the Medical Examiner, Volusia County

Name: UNIDENTIFIED #3.

Age: Race: Black Sex: Male

Case Number 2012-24043

Date (DR) 2/27/2012

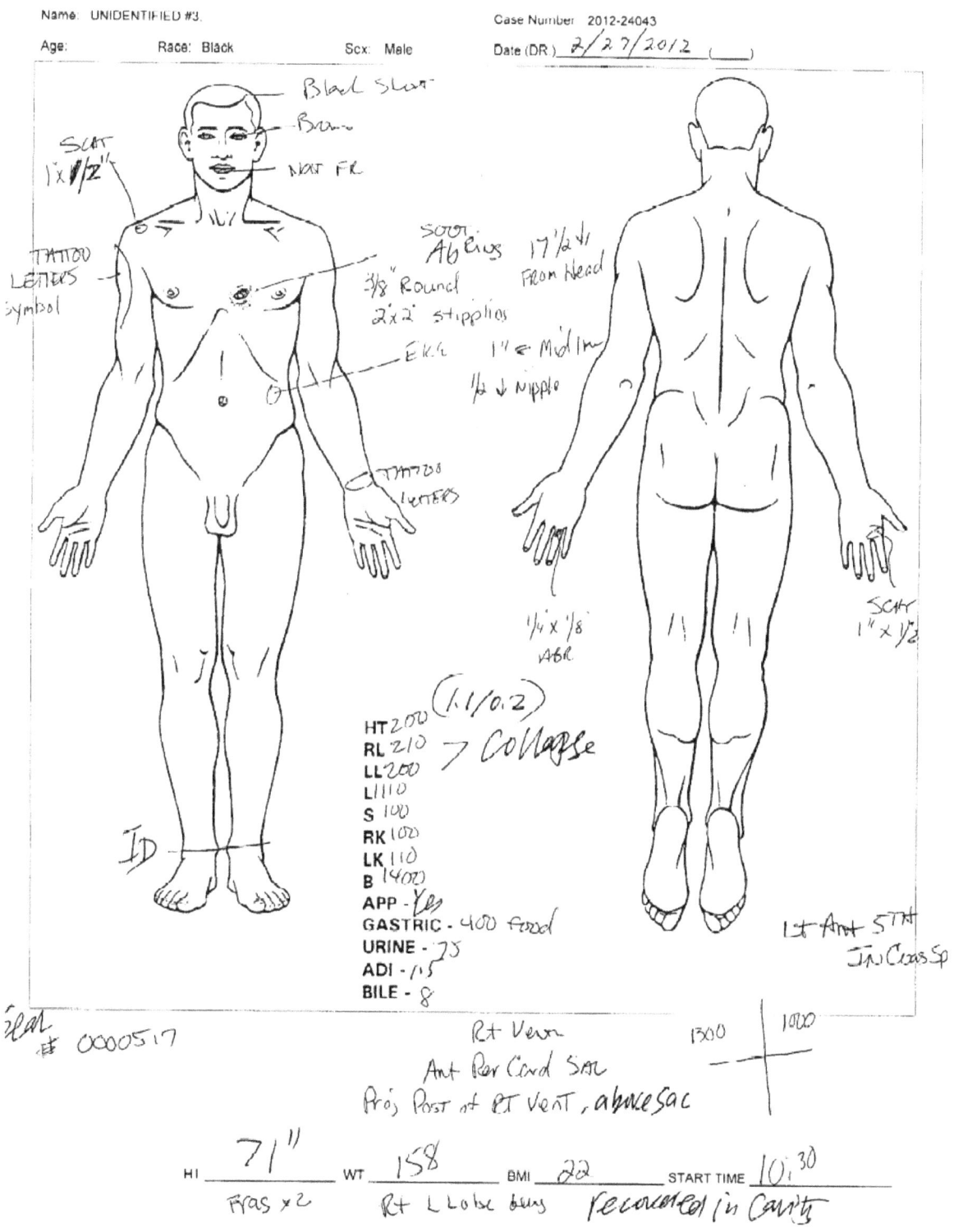

Black Shirt
Brown
Not Fr.

Scar
1" x 1/2"

Tattoo
Letters
Symbol

Scar
Abrasn 17 1/2 ↓
3/8" Round From Head
2 x 2 stipplin
EKG 1" ← Midln
1/2 ↓ Nipple

Tattoo
Letters

1/4 x 1/8
ABR.

SCAR
1" x 1/2"

HT 200 (1.1/0.2)
RL 210 → Collapse
LL 200
LI 110
S 100
RK 100
LK 110
B 1400
APP - Yes
GASTRIC - 400 food
URINE - 75
ADI - 15
BILE - 8

1st Ant 5TH
In Cross Sp

Seal # 0000517

Rt Vein
Ant Per Card Sac
Pro, Post of Rt Vent, above Sac

1300 | 1000

HI __71"__ WT __158__ BMI __22__ START TIME __10:30__
Fras x 2 Rt L Lobe bens Recovered in Cavity

57

knees which would indicate a person kneeling over another person, holding their head in both hands, and slamming it against a hard irregular surface such as a concrete sidewalk.

There were no bruises on either of the forearms inside or out. In other words, there was not a single indication by close examination in the morgue of any corroborating evidence that the victim had been in a fight with another individual.

The heart is tethered to the mediastinum or central core of the chest at the upper portion or base where the aorta and pulmonary arteries are attached but otherwise suspended within the pericardial cavity – the sac surrounding the heart which is filled with fluid – allowing the heart to move freely which is obviously essential since the heart is continuously beating and any attachments would interfere with cardiac function.

Consequently, the heart moves back and forth and side to side constantly and the position of the lower portion, which includes the right and left ventricles in the chest depends upon whether the person is sitting or standing, bending forward or backward, lying on their back or face down.

If Trayvon was on top of the shooter as depicted in the video of the reenactment of the shooting, and since the trajectory is indeed left-to-right, it means that he could not have been reaching across his body, on top of the shooter with his right arm extended to the right hip of the shooter on the ground.

If you're reaching across your body, as previously illustrated, the chest is going to be rotated to the left, and twisted, so a bullet fired from the shooter's right hip area, as was clearly indicated in the video reenactment, the path would actually go into the left lung – the result of the chest being rotated to the left side of the person on top – so the bullet could not go from left-to-right.

However, if the victim is on the ground supine position, the heart is positioned away from the sternum. Allowing rotation that shifts the left ventricle backwards, placing the right ventricle closer to the back of the sternum. The lungs are then shifted toward the top of the chest, placing the lower lobe of the right lung in a direct line with both the right ventricle and the lower left 5th intercostal space.

Analysis of the forensic evidence strongly suggests that the shooter was either standing or kneeling above the victim, who was most likely lying on his back on the ground.

One of the most important tasks for the forensic pathologist is the analysis of injury patterns on the body, with proper evaluation insight is provided into how and when trauma has occurred.

Since pattern analysis can be useful in determining the possible causation of a traumatic injury, it is important to remember that an injury pattern not only involves determining where on the body there is a trauma, but also what areas of the body have been spared.

If presented with a case of a child who had sustained a head injury from a fall down a flight of stairs, and there is only injury to the head itself, the pathologist would question why there were no injuries on other parts of the body. Injuries that would be expected from multiple impacts with the stairs—seriously calling the account of the trauma into question.

Trayvon Martin's autopsy revealed a single injury, consisting of a gunshot wound to the chest. For a teenage boy, allegedly in a physical altercation with an adult male, this absence of any other injuries is particularly unusual in that it would appear he was putting up no resistance, throwing no punches in defense, or in any way defending himself.

This is indeed a rare scenario for a situation in which two individuals are in a serious struggle, one at least in a fight for life, and there is no evidence that any trauma was imparted to the alleged assailant.

This story should have raised red flags because it's about as credible as the case of a child falling down the stairs with no observable injuries other than to his head. Clearly, the mindset that was developed from the start, that Trayvon was the criminal and was shot by another individual in "self-defense," created the bias that resulted in incompetent management of the scene with demonstrable lack of interest in the autopsy. Law enforcement representatives couldn't even manage to show up at the autopsy or properly analyze the findings.

There was an obvious failure to even compare the autopsy findings with the video reconstruction of the events provided by the shooter himself, and basically ignoring all the critical forensic data during the trial.

The real potential for the introduction of bias, even though completely unintended, arises from the fact that LEA investigations tend to be directed toward the finding of a perpetrator, rather than relying on neutral factual data and analysis.

The police are, after all, admittedly a part of the prosecution team and despite their best efforts often come to conclusions that lean toward the prosecutorial side.

While the conclusions drawn from that data may be subject to bias, the actual hard data exists. That data may be independently reviewed by an outside agency, which may subsequently either concur or differ with the initial interpretation. This is supposed to be the job of an independent Medical Examiner.

Second-opinion analysis of the evidentiary data may be very informative and often critical in the development of a legal case, as to what were the actual findings, and how those findings relate to the prosecution's theory of the case.

The prosecution's presentation should never have been accepted at face-value, and the data should be subjected to critical analysis before allowing that data to be presented as scientific fact – particularly in the courtroom.

A further complication may arise, however, in situations wherein an inordinate amount of influence is exercised by the prosecutor, upon the Medical Examiner, to tailor the medical findings to be in concert with their theory of the case being prosecuted.

Many of the conclusions by the Medical Examiner related to the cause, manner, and mechanism of death are dependent upon at least some degree of interpretation of the data generated by the investigation and the autopsy examination. Therefore, any interference with the rendering of an objective, independent opinion, can materially impact the veracity of that opinion.

In the evaluation of Medical Examiner cases, it is imperative to recognize the existence of this potential bias and not assume that the evaluation is completely independent. The reality is that in many instances, a bias (either conscious or not) exists to conform opinions in a way that would be most beneficial to the State.

In most Medical Examiner systems, the State prosecutor and law enforcement have a significant role in choosing the Medical Examiner, and the retention, rejection or employment contracts for the pathologist.

This issue of reluctance of a medical examiner to buck the system, can be illustrated through involvement with a prior case also occurringin Sanford, involving your authors, wherein this problem of bias was exposed.

In this case the doctor had testified that what he thought were multiple cigarette burns on a victim child were identifiable simply by "looking at them." He was apparently trained that this is all a medical examiner needed to do. That was in a case exposing a Defendant to the Death Penalty, so his opinion was welcomed by the State Prosecutor.

However, microscopic evaluation of the tissues presented by the Defense revealed that while the Prosecution and this witness were claiming cigarette burns on the child, there was no subcutaneous thermal changes that would necessarily be present if the burning end of a cigarette had come in contact with the skin. Rather the multiple "wounds" were the result of the child picking at a spreading rash resulting from a skin infection.

That case was prosecuted as a Death Penalty case for two years before the revelation of the error at trial by your authors, Dr. Anderson as an expert witness for the Defense and Cheney Mason as the Defense Attorney. Despite the factual forensic evidence I provided, the Medical Examiner refused to accept the clear evidence I had presented. The State simply responded by attempting to discredit my testimony presented at the trial. Fortunately, the jury was receptive to the facts and the trial ended in an acquittal.

Dr. Shipping Bao was an associated pathologist in a Medical Examiner's office, a foreign medical graduate hired by a Chief Medical Examiner who in turn had been selected several years earlier by the County following the recommendation of a "Search Committee", organized to find a replacement for a recently departed doctor filling that position.

This was a Search Committee that would have, by Florida Statute, consisted of all the Sheriffs, Police Chiefs and State Attorneys from the Judicial Districts of Volusia and Seminole Counties, a single Public Defender, a Single funeral director, and one lay person representing the local community.

The influence of the members from the law enforcement community would vastly outweigh the remaining members simply by numbers alone, if not by the potential intimidating effect of being outnumbered by people in uniforms, wearing badges and carrying guns.

Although the entire Medical Examiner System in Florida is overseen by the Medical Examiner's Commission—a branch of the Florida Department of Law Enforcement—each District in the State chooses their own medical examiner through a local selection committee.

Notably, the entirety of this setup is connected intimately to Law Enforcement and the Prosecutorial branches both locally and at the State level. Thereby putting a considerable amount of pressure on the theoretically independent forensic pathologist to arrive at conclusions supportive to their theories of the cause and manner of death in situations where they are involved.

A former Chief Medical Examiner in Seminole County, the very place where the shooting of Trayvon Martin took place, had once been quoted as saying that "the job of the Medical Examiner is to confirm the theories of Law Enforcement."

Dr. Shiping Bao was understandably not in a position to publicly challenge the accuracy of the events that were unfolding at the local, state, national and ultimately international levels, even if he had been informed about such things as the totally unsubstantiated reconstruction of the shooting upon which the direction of the entire case would be predicated.

He probably didn't want to risk losing his job, and because most other death investigation systems around the country have similar ties with the prosecutorial arm of the government, would most-likely have preferred not taking the risk of becoming essentially unemployable if later blackballed when potential future employers asked the local folks for a reference.

Dr. Anderson, a number of years earlier while applying for a position on the Florida's West Coast, was told by the then head of the Florida Medical Examiner Committee that in order to be successful, I should try to "be warm and fuzzy with law enforcement."

This approach is antithetical to the position that should be the bedrock of the ethical and professional standards of an independent scientist, regardless of their field of endeavor.

As an experienced forensic pathologist being aware of the inherent dangers of such an approach: I wasn't warm and fuzzy....and I didn't get hired.

Following the somewhat disjointed testimony provided by Dr. Bao at the trial, criticism was generated from many sectors. This included inferences by the prosecution, essentially blaming the pathologist for the outcome, which many felt was questionable to say the least. While it is easy to find a scapegoat on the lowest hanging fruit, the Medical Examiner is not the problem here.

It should be pointed out however that the law enforcement team from the very beginning of the investigation at the scene, thru the reenactment of the incident by the shooter, up to and including the basic trial preparation and testimony, there was virtually no attempt by the State Prosecutor to ascertain or utilize the forensic factual data that was generated by the Medical Examiner.

Chapter Six

NO ARREST

Within less than an hour, the news media learned of the shooting and converged on the scene. The reporters were seeking answers and getting none. What was clear is that there was a young Black teenage boy lying on the ground, obviously deceased. The shooter had been removed and was at the Sanford Police Department. He claimed he was attacked by this young victim for no known reason and with no justification.

Under the law, it is clear that "probable cause" may not be established merely on the belief of the arresting officer. If subjective good faith alone were the test, then protections of the Fourth Amendment would evaporate, and people would be secure in their persons, houses, papers, and things only at the discretion of the police. The subjective belief of the police is irrelevant, and probable cause must rest upon a standard that is more objective.

The term "probable cause" and its interpretations have been the subject matter of the courts in this country for decades. The belief of a reasonable police officer is less than that which is required to convict. As the Supreme Court has stated, dealing with probable cause is a matter of dealing with probabilities. Regarding probabilities, more than mere suspicion is less than evidence that would justify conviction. The standard to determine reasonableness to justify arrest includes a determination of the degree of probability.

The facts in this case certainly challenge the interpretation of the police officers in not even disarming, much less arresting Mr. Zimmerman. What is the probability of an unarmed 17-year-old boy attacking without provocation an adult male who is armed? What is the probability of young Trayvon attacking an adult that is unknown to him with no explanation whatsoever?

For the police chief to say that Zimmerman was not arrested because he claimed a defense that he was attacked and therefore, they (the police) had no probable cause to arrest is absurd. It does not meet the standard of reasonableness. What was clearly undisputed is that an unarmed young man was lying on the ground dead with a bullet hole through his chest. What could be probable is that the self-appointed watch commander simply asserted himself without justification to confront a young unknown Black kid wearing a hoodie and it turned into a murder. What actually happened would be up to further investigation and determination by the appropriate authority: the State Attorney.

One might consider that even if young Trayvon had been armed (which he was not) there still would be the issue of whether Mr. Zimmerman was justified in killing him. The assertion of a claim of self-defense is what is known as an "affirmative defense" that he, Zimmerman, would have the burden of establishing. There were no eyewitnesses to support such a defense, nor was there any clear forensic evidence in that regard.

It is a critical point to keep in mind that at no point during these events was any objective forensic evidence being considered. The police trusted the account of the shooting provided by Zimmerman and allowed a video reenactment based upon his word to be produced.

According to documented records from the Medical Examiner and law enforcement agencies, at no point was Dr. Bao or anyone else involved in the actual forensic evidentiary analysis consulted, or even informed as to what was transpiring as this case evolved.

Perhaps, had anyone involved in the legal side of this case bothered to perform even a cursory investigation of the forensic data, the clear discrepancies between the autopsy findings and the shooter's account of events would have been made clear.

Presenting the findings from a woefully incomplete investigation to a Grand Jury would not, in any likelihood, have made any difference. The dye was cast from the beginning and obviously the State and law enforcement were content to proceed based solely on that cursory initial investigation.

Even if by a stretch of imagination there could be a meaningful argument made that the defendant acted in self-defense, a fair and full determination of that could have and should have been presented to a Grand Jury.

On its face, the straightforward and undisputed evidence is that there was an unarmed victim killed by an apparent shot from a gun, and a potential "shooter" standing by with the weapon.

It would indeed be an interesting state of affairs if our system of law enabled the claim of "self-defense" without supporting evidence to dictate how our legal system dealt with the enormous number of homicides in our country.

For those matters that are not so obvious, and coupled with irrefutable evidence, our society utilizes Grand Juries to make objective and fair inquiry. Under Florida Law in all capital cases, a Grand Jury is required before there can be formal charges filed against the accused actor.

In this case, due to there being the absence of any "irrefutable evidence" of the innocence of or justification for the actions of Mr. Zimmerman, a Grand Jury should have been convened.

Had young Trayvon Martin been lying on the ground with a gun in his hand and some evidence of having used that or threatened to use that against Zimmerman, then that could be a different story.

But there was no such evidence. There was simply the unsupported story by Mr. Zimmerman that this teenager had, for no apparent reason, attacked him and therefore was justified in being shot.

If the State Attorney for Seminole County had objectively reviewed the undisputed "facts", he should have convened a Grand Jury. A Grand Jury is an independent body of citizens comprised of fifteen to twenty-one people who receive evidence confidentially and the testimony and outcomes are recorded.

There are extensive procedures in Florida, as in all other jurisdictions in this country, to present issues of fact and questions to the Grand Jury who then decide whether there is sufficient evidence to render a conviction.

They have the right to determine that, as asserted in this case, Mr. Zimmerman was justified in shooting this unarmed teenager, or they could have found that Zimmerman was acting out of racial bias and on non-existent authority.

No Grand Jury was ever given the chance or opportunity to review the "evidence" and render such a decision objectively and independently. The State Attorney for the Circuit did not even suggest the use of a Grand Jury. He did not even convene an inquiry about the evidence.

If the State Attorney had done what should have been done in this type of circumstance, he would have convened a Grand Jury to evaluate the facts of the case. Mr. Zimmerman, together with his chosen lawyer, could appear before the Grand Jury to answer their questions.

He could have presented to the Grand Jury his claim of "self-defense." Had that been done, the Grand Jury could have rendered an Indictment against him charging him with Capital First Degree Murder. Remember, he shot an unarmed victim with no justifying evidence readily apparent or witnesses to support such a claim.

The Grand Jury could have also decided to charge Mr. Zimmerman with lesser criminal offenses such as Second-Degree Murder, Manslaughter, Aggravated Assault with a Firearm, and others.

They would have had the opportunity to question Mr. Zimmerman if he did not assert his 5th Amendment protections, together with reviewing the undisputed physical evidence. They then could have rendered what is known as a "no bill." That is to decline to charge Mr. Zimmerman with any criminal act whatsoever. The case would then have been over.

Uniquely in this case and the entire scenario, we have a recorded reenactment video production by the Defendant. Reviewing the role of that reenactment leaves substantial questions about the workings of our country's judicial system in this case.

Notwithstanding the undisputed fact of the shooting of an unarmed kid with no defense witnesses, Mr. Zimmerman was not even charged until six weeks later after significant public outcry. The case was never presented to a Grand Jury for independent and objective evaluation.

A review of that self-serving reenactment video with the undisputed forensic evidence presented here points to a large number of dramatic inconsistencies, if not outright falsehoods asserted by the shooter.

Zimmerman attempted to justify his own actions by asserting what has unfortunately become a typical story of racial bias. When he performed for his own self-defense reenactment, he claimed that the victim was seen with his hands in his waistband while there is clear evidence that shows he was on the phone with a female friend in Miami.

During the long hiatus between the killing and the formal charge, there were numerous news broadcasts dealing with the case both locally and nationally.

In many of those broadcasts, based upon interviews of the law enforcment community and documents, it was revealed that Zimmerman was immediately and preferentially taken from the crime scene. He was not subjected to any form of toxicology test to determine the potential presence and influence of alcohol or drugs.

Apparently, they didn't even do a background check on him.

KATHLEEN FLYNN | Times

Benjamin Jealous, president of the National Association for the Advancement of Colored People, speaks at a town hall meeting Tuesday on the slaying of Trayvon Martin. More than 350 people packed into Allen Chapel AME Church.

She told Crump that Martin said he was being followed.

"Run!" she recalled telling him. "Trayvon said he's not running."

Crump said phone records back up the girl's story showing that the "suspicious" person who neighborhood watch thought was "up to no good" was simply a teen like any other.

"This girl connects the dots," said Crump, who added he plans to turn the tape over to federal investigators, but not to Sanford police.

Attorneys for Martin's family accuse the Sanford police of protecting Zimmerman because he shares their love for law enforcement.

Zimmerman, who was born in Virginia and studied criminal justice at Seminole State College, is the son of a retired Virginia Supreme Court magistrate and his wife, a longtime

clerk of courts, according to his application to the citizen's academy.

Sanford police released a log of Zimmerman's dozens of calls to police dating back to 2004, which show a pattern of his reporting suspicious people and minor nuisances.

Zimmerman was arrested in a scuffle with an undercover officer in 2005, but the charges were dropped when he entered a pretrial diversion program that allowed him to have a clean record.

When he applied for the citizen's police academy, Zimmerman insisted he did not know the man he scuffled with was a cop.

"I hold law enforcement officers in the highest regaurd [sic] as I hope to one day become one," he wrote in his application. "I would never have touched a police officer."

tionally black neighborhood of Sanford. A line flowed down steps with others trying to get in.

Civil rights leaders from the NAACP, ACLU and the Nation of Islam urged residents to remain calm but demand that George Zimmerman be arrested. They also said the town's police chief should step down.

"I stand here as a son, father, uncle who is tired of being scared for our boys," said Benjamin Jealous, national president of the NAACP. "I'm tired of telling our young men how they can't dress, where they can't go and how they can't behave."

Residents attending the meeting cheered and jumped to their feet when local NAACP leader Turner Clayton Jr. said the U.S. Department of Justice shouldn't just review the investigation but the federal agency also should take over the Sanford Police Department.

"This is just the beginning of what is taking place," Clayton said. "We're going to make sure justice prevails."

Associated Press

Tampa Bay Times, St. Pete, Wed., March 21, 2012

67

In other words, a police officer at the scene decided that despite the undisputed evidence of the victim and the shooting, that he, the officer, was both the judge and jury on the spot.

The evidence, or rather the lack thereof, further indicates that the judgment by the police carried on for weeks. As seen above, there was apparently no effort to try to collect or identify any forensic evidence of the crime scene, i.e., the sidewalk or any weapons.

Even though there was a witness describing what was heard and partially seen of Zimmerman's unusual behavior after the shot was fired, there was no effort made to determine whether Mr. Zimmerman inflicted the superficial wounds on his scalp himself.

In his realization of what he had just done, he could very easily, given the training he had received, struck himself on the scalp with either the butt of his murder weapon pistol, or his cell phone.

Despite the detectives' having access to both those items, there is no documentation that either was examined or tested for blood or DNA, which would seem to be the logical first step in a properly managed forensic investigation.

A significant and critical additional question comes from the failure of the prosecution to search recent phone calls made by Trayvon Martin. In fact, it was only after the initial accusations that the lawyer representing Trayvon's family was able to determine that at the very instant of the shooting, Trayvon was talking on his phone to the young lady in Miami.

That fact would have been critical to prove time, duration, and subject of his phone conversation. Later, as will be seen, the young woman testified that she was talking to Trayvon, he was calling for help, complaining that some "cracker" was following him, and he was afraid.

Chapter Seven

7

BLACK LIVES MATTER

Despite the significant conflicts in evidence weighed against the unrefuted fact of the cause and manner of death to young Trayvon Martin, the police persisted in their refusal to make an arrest. The result of this caused an almost unprecedented public outcry, both locally and nationally. In fact, this case and the facts surrounding the action and inaction resulted in the now well-established mantra of "Black Lives Matter."

It was frequently suggested by celebrities and politicians that had the roles been reversed, there would have been an immediate arrest and prosecution. The news of the apparent racial bias and handling of this case invoked significant objections from the public in general.

Trayvon was killed on the early evening of February 26, 2012. There was no question as to who did it, as Mr. George Zimmerman did not flee the scene, but rather stayed waiting for the police to arrive.

Notwithstanding the fact that Zimmerman was unquestionably the shooter and that the victim, Trayvon Martin, was unarmed, the police did not make the arrest. The authors have been able to ascertain that the police did little, if any further investigation, into the incident for a virtually unprecedented time for a Homicide case—nearly six weeks.

Zimmerman had been told by the police not to follow Martin and that they were on the way in response to Zimmerman's call suggesting a suspicious stranger in the neighborhood. No details were provided, but it started the fire that grew into a national incident.

One of first major concerns related to the failure to arrest came from the "New Black Panther Party." Being aware of the skimpy news reports in the first several days, the Black Panthers joined the outcry for arrest.

They gathered in front of the Sanford Police Department headquarters demanding the arrest of Zimmerman. All that was known at that time was that at the time of the shooting there had been several citizens making 911 calls about people fighting in the courtyard of the condominiums.

The national news media was rapidly increasing its coverage revealing the circumstances of the shooting of Trayvon. As a result of the expanding national news coverage, Zimmerman's phone was disconnected. There were growing protests in cities all over the country.

Trayvon's parents held a news conference, because they were concerned about nothing being done to seek justice for the murder of their son. Despite the passage of weeks, there was no arrest.

Benjamin Crump, a nationally renowned civil rights lawyer, was helping the victim's parents in their quest for justice. He filed a lawsuit to get a copy of the 911 calls that had been made before Trayvon was killed, but the police declined the request.

Among the public outcry were the concerns as to why the shooter, Zimmerman, had not even been arrested. There never was a question that it was he who did the shooting and that the victim was unarmed. Nor was there any question about the victim's innocence: no allegations of any wrongdoing; no claims of criminal activity; no claims of trespass, maliciousness, or any illegal behavior.

It is also clear that part of the main concern was not just that Zimmerman was not even arrested, but that he was a "White man acting like a cop" and the victim was a "Black teenager."

The Chief of Police in Sanford had publicly stated that Zimmerman was "squeaky clean" and had a clean record criminally. This was proven to be false.

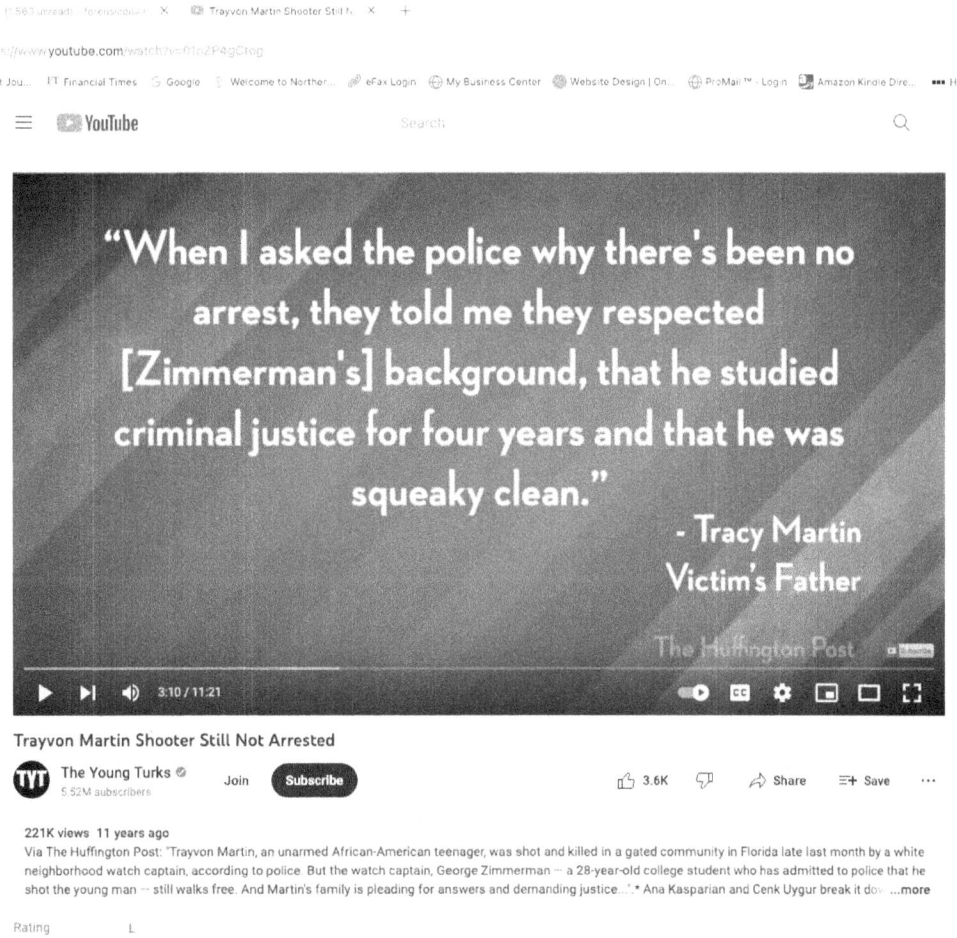

In fact, Mr. Zimmerman was known to the police in Sanford. He had previously been arrested and charged with assaulting a police officer.

He was later allowed to enter a plea bargain that resulted in a probationary sentence, and he was not formally convicted, thus causing the lack of a formal record. It was the same police department that now was hiding their inaction and failure to arrest on the obviously fraudulent claim that Zimmerman was squeaky clean.

In virtually every similar type of situation, no matter where it may have occurred, there clearly was probable cause to believe that Zimmerman had killed this young man who was unarmed. He could have justifiably questioned him on trespassing, but there were no actions taken by Trayvon that warranted an arrest, much less a shooting.

The initial analysis on the part of law enforcement was that because Zimmerman had claimed self-defense that they, the police, didn't feel like there was enough evidence to arrest for wrongdoing. The Sanford Police Chief defended the department's actions by claiming that Mr. Zimmerman had a "squeaky clean background."

Over several years before this shooting, Mr. Zimmerman had been involved in numerous confrontations with citizens without any official or lawful process to confront them. This would suggest a pattern of confrontations with people who were, at worst, taking a shortcut through the community or trespassing.

In 2005, Mr. Zimmerman was arrested for entering a struggling confrontation with a police officer. Alleging that he "didn't know it was a police officer", he ultimately was allowed to enter a plea bargain and enter a Pretrial Diversion Program. As a result of that the charges were dropped against him, thus he had a "clean record" (See clipping on next page).

The physical confronting of any individuals or "suspicious people" is in direct violation of the guidelines for the Neighborhood Watch Program and would constitute poor judgment on the part of any individual acting in that manner.

The National Sheriff's Association has published a manual for Neighborhood Watch volunteers. The manual specifically states the following: "What you will not do is get physically involved with any activity you report or apprehension of any suspicious persons. This is the job of the law enforcement agency." Also, additional directives such as, "Neighborhood Watch" is an observe-and-report type program. Neighborhood Watch members are encouraged not to stop and question people, but to observe and report their observations to the Sheriff's Office and a trained officer would respond and investigate."

Further, the manual states, "It should be emphasized to members that they do not possess police powers, and they shall not carry weapons or pursue vehicles. They should also be cautioned to alert police or deputies in encountering strange activities. Members should never confront suspicious person who could be armed and dangerous."

KATHLEEN FLYNN | Times

Benjamin Jealous, president of the National Association for the Advancement of Colored People, speaks at a town hall meeting Tuesday on the slaying of Trayvon Martin. More than 350 people packed into Allen Chapel AME Church.

Benjamin Crump, the attorney for the dead teen's family, said the incident was another disturbing development in a case riddled with police missteps. He was also troubled by the decision to take the case to a grand jury, which meets in private.

If the roles had been reversed "would Trayvon Martin have gotten the courtesy of a grand jury?" Crump asked. "Whatever case they put out, we won't know. They can come out — and say 'It wasn't us, it was the community.'"

Crump, who is based in Tallahassee, flew to Miami after Martin's father combed through his son's cell phone records and discovered he was on the telephone moments before he died.

The number belonged to a girl Martin had spent hours talking to that weekend, a girl he was dating. Crump recorded her statement and played it for reporters at a news conference Tuesday in Fort Lauderdale. He said he promised the girl's parents he would not reveal her name.

Records show she called Martin at 7:12 p.m. and spoke to him for four minutes. Zimmerman's call to police was at 7:11.

She told Crump that Martin said he was being followed.

"Run!" she recalled telling him. "Trayvon said he's not running."

Crump said phone records back up the girl's story, showing that the "suspicious" person who neighborhood watch thought was "up to no good" was simply a teen like any other.

"This girl connects the dots," said Crump, who added he plans to turn the tape over to federal investigators, but not to Sanford police.

Attorneys for Martin's family accuse the Sanford police of protecting Zimmerman because he shares their love for law enforcement.

Zimmerman, who was born in Virginia and studied criminal justice at Seminole State College, is the son of a retired Virginia Supreme Court magistrate and his wife, a longtime clerk of courts, according to his application to the citizen's academy.

Sanford police released a log of Zimmerman's dozens of calls to police dating back to 2004, which show a pattern of his reporting suspicious people and minor nuisances.

Zimmerman was arrested in a scuffle with an undercover officer in 2005, but the charges were dropped when he entered a pretrial diversion program that allowed him to have a clean record.

When he applied for the citizen's police academy, Zimmerman insisted he did not know the man he scuffled with was a cop.

"I hold law enforcement officers in the highest regaurd [sic] as I hope to one day become one," he wrote in his application. "I would never have touched a police officer."

day, more than 350 people packed into the wood paneled sanctuary of the Allen Chapel AME Church, located in a traditionally black neighborhood of Sanford. A line flowed down steps with others trying to get in.

Civil rights leaders from the NAACP, ACLU and the Nation of Islam urged residents to remain calm but demand that George Zimmerman be arrested. They also said the town's police chief should step down.

"I stand here as a son, father, uncle who is tired of being scared for our boys," said Benjamin Jealous, national president of the NAACP. "I'm tired of telling our young men how they can't dress, where they can't go and how they can't behave."

Residents attending the meeting cheered and jumped to their feet when local NAACP leader Turner Clayton Jr. said the U.S. Department of Justice shouldn't just review the investigation but the federal agency also should take over the Sanford Police Department.

"This is just the beginning of what is taking place," Clayton said. "We're going to make sure justice prevails."

Associated Press

Clearly Zimmerman revealed his total disregard of such directives, and his characterization of Trayvon Martin as "suspect" in his handwritten account given to the police contradicts any suggestion that he considered his role only as a passive observer, reporting suspicious incidents to the proper authorities.

Astonishingly, the Chief of Police in Sanford, Bill Lee, stated that no arrest was made because they did not have probable cause to arrest him.

Conflicting news reports reveal that the shooter was claimed to be innocent by his father. Of course, his father was not on the scene and could not have any knowledge about anything other than the stories given to him by his son. There were several witnesses with conflicting versions of what happened.

One of the witnesses insisted that the police were not paying any attention to her. She said that she saw the fight and that there was no punching or hitting. She and other witnesses heard someone repeatedly crying for help, followed instantly by a single gunshot.

73

IN HIS OWN WORDS From George Zimmerman's handwritten statement of events to Sanford police the night of the shooting.

fired one shot into his torso. The suspect sat back allowing me to sit up and said "You got me."

ZIMMERMAN'S ACCOUNT

FROM THE VIDEO: ZIMMERMAN RE-ENACTS SHOOTING FOR POLICE

Zimmerman tells police he was on his way to Target and saw a person standing in the rain near the town house he is pointing at. "There's been a history of break-ins in that building."

In this photo, captured from the video re-enactment, bandages are visible on the back of Zimmerman's head. He is describing the moments before his confrontation with Trayvon Martin.

THE QUESTIONING
Portions of Sanford police Investigator Chris Serino's Feb. 29 interview of Zimmerman:

INVESTIGATOR
You essentially saw somebody who you in good faith thought was doing something wrong.

INVESTIGATOR
Ever hear of Murphy's Law?

ZIMMERMAN
Yes, sir.

INVESTIGATOR
OK, that's what happened. **This person was not doing anything bad. He was 17 years old. An athlete. A kid with a future.** A kid with folks that care. ... Not the goon.

INVESTIGATOR
You have any prior training in law enforcement at all? As far as identifying people, what to look for that makes them really suspicious?

INVESTIGATOR
If you guys continue Neighborhood Watch, typically the garb is black on black on black with a black hoodie. This guy had a gray hoodie. But his pants were beige. Not exactly your prime-suspect type.

Video re-enactment, recordings, voice-stress test among releases

BY RENE STUTZMAN AND JEFF WEINER
Staff Writers

The day after he killed Trayvon Martin, an unflappable George Zimmerman with bandages on his head walked down the side-

re-enactment: Zimmerman said he didn't know at first that his single shot had struck Trayvon. He said the teen sat up after the blast and said, "You got me," but Zimmerman took that to mean Trayvon was giving up.

Before the shot, Zimmerman

The question seems obvious: Why would Zimmerman call for help since he was the adult armed with a 9 mm semi-automatic pistol? He had reported the presence of a stranger by calling the police who said they were on the way and advised him to remain in his vehicle and not follow the "suspect."

One of the key witnesses, apparently ignored by the Prosecutor, was one of the neighbors who made it known that she saw and heard what was going on. She told the police that she saw Zimmerman right after the shooting standing there with both of his hands waving over his head and gesturing as if he was acknowledging he had really done something he regretted.

Over the couple of weeks after the shooting, the police were receiving thousands of contacts demanding an arrest and prosecution. The NAACP, along with a number of other civil rights organizations, took great interest in the killing of Trayvon. They made a demand that the Sanford Police Chief, who had claimed to not have any probable cause to arrest the shooter, be fired.

As reported by numerous sources, it is clear that if Zimmerman had followed the directions from the police and not pursued this unknown teenager who was doing nothing illegal and waited for the police who were slightly over a minute away, there would have been no shooting and Trayvon would be alive.

74

Chapter Eight

THE HOODIE

As the days carried on with no action taken, a wide outcry arose calling not only for the firing of the Chief of Police, but the hiring and appointing of a new Prosecutor. While the demands grew, and the voices got louder, still no action was taken by the Sanford Police; no action was taken by the prosecuting attorney; no action was taken by any level of government.

After repeated demands, threats, and demonstrations, the Sanford Chief of Police took an easy way out. Approximately four weeks after the shooting he resigned his position.

As a result, demonstrations and demands rapidly increased. Well-known national civil rights leader, Reverend Al Sharpton, got involved. He arrived at downtown Sanford to protest the way the killing was being handled. He was joined by an estimated eight thousand people in a widely publicized rally.

Many of the demonstrators came wearing hoodies. The rally, attended and led by the Reverend Sharpton was twenty-six days after the shooting. During this time nothing had been done by the police or the Prosecutor.

It was a fact that Trayvon Martin was wearing a "hoodie" at the time of the shooting. Apparently, there was a segment of our society that associated the wearing of a hoodie as some kind of symbol of "thuggery" or criminal act. Apparently, the phone conversation with the police dispatcher described a "suspicious" person as wearing a hoodie.

It became clear that a substantial percentage of our society associated the wearing of a "hoodie" with not only some criminal thuggery, but also a racial identity point. Mr. Martin's family and others urged supporters in favor of an arrest and prosecution to join in a protest planned for New York City.

This was to be a "Million Hoodie March" to protest the failure to arrest. The supporters were urged to wear hoodies and pull the hoods over their heads during the March. It was acknowledged by many of the protest leaders that if the hoodie was worn by someone older or whiter, it would be clear that a hoodie was only a commonly worn sweatshirt.

Numerous celebrity stars, including film maker Spike Lee, movie celebrities like MC Hammer and Mia Farrow, and other concerned citizens of all races joined in the protest supporting the outcry to arrest Zimmerman.

The victim's parents launched a petition on the internet and almost immediately had over six hundred and fifteen thousand signatures.

The turmoil created by the initial reports reached as far as the elite basketball player, LeBron James, of the Miami Heat. The concern for Trayvon Martin's death and the lack of arrest was so impactful that the members of the Miami Heat painted their shoes with "Rest in Peace Trayvon Martin" and "We Want Justice."

As part of the outcry and growing wave of demands for tha arrest of Mr. Zimmerman, the Black Panther Party offered a $10,000 reward for the "capture" of Zimmerman. This action prompted Reverend Jesse Jackson to become visibly involved. He reported that if the police did their job there would be no need for the growing number of protests.

Geraldo Rivera got involved and spoke out about judging people as criminals based on what clothes they chose to wear. He opined publicly after the shooting, and prior to the arrest, that he did not believe the shooter would have responded as he did if Trayvon had not been wearing a hoodie.

The Champion company first produced sweatshirts with hoodies back in the 1930s. They were for workers having to work in freezing New York warehouses.

Later in the 70s, hoodies popularity exploded in the "hip-hop and graffiti culture." It was also apparently reported in places outside of the U.S., like the United Kingdom that the hoodie had jumped from a social statement to a social stigma.

Some malls and schools banned hoodies which had become known as the unofficial uniform of petty thieves and hooligans. Police in Brisbane, Australia urged shopkeepers to have "hoodie-free zones." Stores like Target, Abercrombie & Fitch, and Old Navy at the time sold hoodies adorned with patriotic flags for the 4th of July, others with cat ears, some with fur, and even some with dinosaur spikes. The city of New York even sold police department hoodies.

The world was essentially captivated by the killing of Trayvon Martin. A Texas based group called National Association for Legal Gun Defense offered to put up $10,000.00 to help pay for Zimmerman's expenses. At the same time, more than two million people signed a Petition on Change.org asking for justice.

All these events happened more than a week before Zimmerman was finally arrested. In Sanford, the police department had pronounced that they would arrest any members of the media who asked city employees questions off the record about the incident. When that action was revealed to the public the order was changed.

Demonstrations were so prolific that the Chief Judge of Seminole County ordered protesters to remain at least a hundred feet away from the front door of the courthouse. Protest marchers appeared in Tallahassee in memory of Trayvon Martin on the 44th anniversary of the assassination of the Reverend Martin Luther King, Jr. Most of those marching and protesting wore hoodies.

The issue of race took over and dominated most of the news. Analyses of the racial biases that led to the murder of Trayvon and preferential treatment of Zimmerman were being made not only by reporters but by many citizens in general. People began to take sides based on the growing racial conflict. The fact is that law enforcement officers participated in racially motivated behavior.

77

The Orlando Sentinel (Orlando, Florida) · Sun, Apr 14, 2013 · Page B3
Downloaded on Jun 20, 2025

Local briefing

Officer fired for Trayvon target practice

A Port Canaveral police sergeant was fired Friday after an internal investigation showed he offered other officers a target resembling Trayvon Martin to use for shooting practice. Sgt. Ron King, a two-year veteran of the force of about 35 sworn officers, offered the target of a hoodie-wearing Trayvon at the range near Cocoa on April 4, Rosalind Harvey, a port spokeswoman, said Saturday. The other officers, who were on duty, refused. King led firearms classes at the range, Harvey said. Port Canaveral Interim Chief Executive Officer John Walsh apologized publicly to Trayvon's family Saturday. "Whether his [King's] act is one of hatred or stupidity, neither one is tolerable," Walsh said. "Using a dead child's image as target practice is reprehensible," said Benjamin Crump, an attorney representing Trayvon's parents.

Susan Jacobson

The Orlando Sentinel (Orlando, Florida) · Fri, Apr 5, 2013 · Page B2
Downloaded on Jun 20, 2025

Winter Park police lieutenant retires under pressure after racial remark

A Winter Park police lieutenant retired Thursday rather than be fired after an investigation found he made a racially derogatory remark against blacks.

Lt. Ron Johnson, 48, made the remark while speaking to fellow officers at the end of a day-shift briefing in February when the topic of the Trayvon Martin shooting came up. "This is why they should be drowned at birth," Johnson said, in an apparent reference to black people.

"The intention of Johnson's comment was clearly understood to be racially derogatory," read the complaint filed March 8 by Officer Paul Foster.

The investigation confirmed the accusation against Johnson, a 27-year veteran of the department.

David Breen

A sergeant with the police department in Port Canaveral, Florida set up a target resembling Trayvon Martin to be used by the officers in their shooting practice. Fortunately, the officer was fired, but the reality of the issue of race in this widespread upheaval became apparent. Counter demonstrations began with the slogan "White Lives Matter" as the organizing theme.

Not to be outdone, a lieutenant from the Winter Park Police Department retired instead of being fired because of comments that he made. While speaking to fellow officers about the Trayvon Martin shooting, he was quoted as saying: "This is why they should be drowned at birth", referring to Black people.

78

In the American South, county and state slave-catching forces arose to **pursue runaway slaves**, a precursor to organized police departments.

— www.historycollection.com

There are many documented and undocumented examples of this way of looking at upholding the laws of our local, state, and federal levels of government. We have chosen only two instances to illustrate the fact that this mindset exists on the part of some of those in authority who have sworn to uphold our laws and protect our citizenry.

The concept of police agencies was born in the Antebellum South for the purpose of tracking down run-away slaves. Apparently, some vestiges of their origin persists in some dark corners continuing to the present day.

Even in the trial, the jury was allowed to hear the recorded phone calls from Zimmerman to the police just prior to the shooting. He advised the police on at least four different occasions when he was reporting suspicious persons that the suspect was Black. That's when he also added the comment "these assholes, they always get away."

Star celebrities like basketball legend LeBron James and others publicly expressed their dismay with the failure of the killer of Trayvon Martin to be brought to justice. Reverend Al Sharpton condemned the non-action to arrest Zimmerman. Public demonstrations occurred around the country, revealing the overwhelming sentiment that it was wrong to just summarily excuse Zimmerman without even having him face a jury, but their cries were ignored.

During this time Oprah Winfrey expressed deep sadness over the Trayvon Martin case, calling it a tragedy and emphasized the need for open conversations about race and justice in America. She hosted conversations and interviews, contributing to a broader dialogue on the case and its impact on society.

She conducted interviews with Trayvon Martin's family creating a space to discuss their feelings and experiences. It wasn't just about the legal aspects; it was focused on understanding the broader issues that the case brought to light.

Stories, questions, and exasperation were evident from numerous national television show publications in addition to virtually all the newspapers in the country. This unjustified killing of Trayvon Martin "lit the fuse" to review the ongoing, and in some cases increasing, racial prejudice in this country.

The outcry was so intense that when the matter was presented to then President of the United States, Barack Obama, he expressed serious concern that the unjustified shooting with Trayvon as the victim, could have been he, the President, as the victim.

Further, the Attorney General of the United States, Mr. Eric Holder expressed great concern for the privileged treatment Zimmerman received despite the undisputed fact that he killed this 17-year-old unarmed kid, for no apparent reason. It is worth reiterating there never was any form of allegation that young Trayvon Martin had done anything wrong whatsoever to even justify confrontation by Zimmerman.

After the public outcry and condemnations from politicians, star athletes, and hundreds of thousands of citizens, finally something was done. Political leaders from across the country put so much pressure on then Florida Governor Rick Scott that he realized that he needed to take action. Federal authorities requested the United States Justice Department get involved in the inquiry.

As a result of this pressure, Governor Scott then appointed a special prosecutor to inquire about the case. There was no need or justification to use a special prosecutor. Local resources were available to manage all the legal requirements. All that they needed was for the elected Prosecutor in the circuit of this crime to do his job.

Instead of the matter being administered using standard established procedures in the ordinary course of events, as it should have been, Governor Scott appointed an out-of-district prosecutor to inquire about the case. Even so, no Grand Jury was convened to make an objective and independent inquiry.

The newly appointed State Attorney simply filed criminal charges on her own authority to accuse Mr. Zimmerman of Second-Degree Murder. As a matter of law, that should have required evaluation of evidence of either mutual combat or some other defense to benefit Zimmerman.

This whole process escalated to such news prominence that the issue of race could not be avoided. Moreover, without any justification, it appeared that the decision to arrest or not arrest had both political support and opposition.

There were various polls taken regarding this case and according to CNN as well as others, two-thirds of the citizens polled wanted Zimmerman to be arrested but one-third didn't. When the polls were further analyzed, it turned out that only 25% of the Republicans supported the arrest of Zimmerman. Democrats overwhelmingly wanted him to be arrested. This was the political environment that existed at the time of the trial.

Chapter Nine

STAND YOUR GROUND DEFENSE

The "Stand Your Ground" law became a major issue in the outcry at the time of the arrest of Zimmerman in the murder of Trayvon Martin. The law used to be that a person was required to retreat from confrontations and violence if they had the ability to safely retreat and were not the initiator of the wrongdoing. However, in 2005 the Florida Law was changed and was thereafter known as the "Stand Your Ground Law."

What it means is that an individual has no duty to retreat and has the right to stand his or her ground and meet force with force, including deadly force, if he or she reasonably believes it is necessary to do so to prevent death or great bodily harm to themself or another, or to prevent the commission of a forcible felony. The result of this change in law now allows someone to protect themselves from wrongful conduct in these situations.

Regardless of various side claims of racism and other activities, the undisputed facts are that Mr. Zimmerman did not know Trayvon Martin. Zimmerman was armed with a 9 mm pistol, Martin was unarmed. Martin was committing no crime or wrongdoing of any kind; Zimmerman had reported a "suspicious character" to the police department but was told by the police to not follow this identified person.

Throughout the investigation of this case and its history, the validity of the "Stand Your Ground Law" was constantly debated. To open the discussion, one had to assume that somehow, and for some reason, Mr. Trayvon Martin must have attacked Zimmerman. Despite both being mutually unknown to the other and Trayvon being unarmed, the assertion is that with the confrontation Zimmerman was entitled to defend himself and not flee.

A clear explanation of this was presented by one of the most respected jurists in the state of Florida, Circuit Judge Milton Hirsch. He elucidated as follows: "In ordinary circumstances a push or a slap may be met with a push or a slap or perhaps a punch, but not with a bullet."

Complicating the issue in this case is the fact that the victim was not doing anything except walking home from a convenience store with his Skittles and his iced tea.

On the other hand, Zimmerman armed himself, described himself on the scene to the police, with a body on the ground, as "watch commander" for the Neighborhood Watch program. Having seen nothing other than a person walking, even at worst case, a trespasser, and had been told not to follow him. He ignored those instructions, clearly articulated by the dispatcher, deciding to handle the situation on his own.

The law is one of self-defense. Nowhere does it say that a person has a right to confront another. When Zimmerman ignored the police directions, he lost that right of self-defense. He had no right to pursue young Trayvon and that by doing so, carrying the gun would legally be considered a premeditated criminal act.

All the interpretations of law cannot and do not challenge the obvious logic. Zimmerman confronted, Zimmerman was armed, Zimmerman shot him, Trayvon died. Hypothetically, if Zimmerman had confronted this young man and identified himself as a watch commander patrolling the neighborhood, showed some credentials, and began to ask questions, then some level of a defense could be raised.

None of this is alleged to have happened.

Zimmerman's story is simply that the kid walked up to him, hit him in the nose, knocked him down (it is highly unlikely given the relative strength and sizes of the two people) and then beat Zimmerman's head against the sidewalk forcing him to draw his gun to save his life by murdering the kid. It appears to be a totally made-up story, illogical and not born out by any witness testimony or forensic evidence.

Politicians not only around the state of Florida, but the entire country, had different opinions to express about this case. None of whom, however, were witnesses that knew exactly what did or did not happen. What we do know is that there is no one to corroborate a first punch confrontation. Further, as Judge Hirsch stated, it is not a legitimate Stand Your Ground situation to return a punch with a bullet.

The law and procedures in Florida since the creation of this "Stand Your Ground Law" provides that an accused person can assert that the law is applicable by filing a Motion making such a claim. A hearing would then be held (not a jury trial) with the appropriate Court.

If the Defendant presented the evidence to support his claim of lawful self-defense, then the Court could grant that Defendant immunity and thus end the prosecution. In this case, despite all the press back and forth, the strategic statements, the Motions and arguments, the Defense never filed such a Motion.

The defense lawyers appeared to be unquestionably, and frankly inexplicably, ahead of the Prosecution. Zimmerman's lawyers knew that to seek the so-called "immunity" they would have to put him on the witness stand where he would then be confronted and cross-examined. That would of course open the full challenge to Zimmerman through forensic evidence.

Notwithstanding the above, for many months the debate was repeatedly held in political circles in the State of Florida, to determine the validity of the Stand Your Ground Law and whether it should be continued or repealed. There was such discussion and concern about this that the then Florida Governor appointed a task force to investigate the validity of the Stand Your Ground Law.

A group of some fifty plus Black lawyers had presented this concern to the Governor seeking such an investigation. United States Representative Alcee Hastings stated that he had great concern about the Stand Your Ground Law and that it in essence is a license to kill.

Another U.S. Representative, Alan West, revealed his position that Zimmerman should have, of course, been arrested and in custody, not allowed to be walking around uncharged and carrying a concealed weapon. His opinion was that Zimmerman had no probable cause to arrest or even engage Trayvon Martin and certainly not justification to pursue him and shoot him.

Following the shooting and up until the eventual trial, the Defense continued to suggest that they may rely upon the "Stand Your Ground" defense and that Zimmerman was entitled to it. Yet, no Motion was filed.

The subject of the "Stand Your Ground Law" also became significant at the time of trial. National news commentators had varying opinions. One was the assertion by Zimmerman that he had lied about claiming to have no knowledge of the Stand Your Ground Law. Zimmerman had previously been interviewed on Fox News by Sean Hannity concerning his knowledge of the law.

In fact, Zimmerman had been studying about that law at Seminole State College. Zimmerman was exposed as having been educated about the law despite thinking it was clearly in his best interest to deny having any knowledge of it at all.

He denied he knew about the law publicly on national TV, but it was eventually revealed that he did. It was just another example of the way he changed his story when it suited him.

Stand your ground was, in this case, a convenient smokescreen that the Defense utilized to keep the State and the press pre-occupied to the point that they failed to recognize some of the real issues involved in this situation.

That the prosecution took the bait so easily reflects either an astonishingly level of incompetence, or more likely a deliberate effort to cloud the issues and in doing so themselves create reasonable doubt!

Chapter Ten

10

ABOUT THE LAWYERS

Most people believe that the United States Constitution provides for every person accused of a crime to have a lawyer. In reality, it is not so simple. It was a succession of interpretations of the Constitution that has evolved into what is now commonly known as a "right to counsel."

In fact, for decades there was no "right to counsel." This didn't really come into play until 1966. People in this country, and apparently many other jurisdictions, have come to accept a belief that automatically persons accused of crimes are entitled to a lawyer.

The Miranda v. Arizona Decision of the United States Supreme Court, together with two other Decisions at the same time, did not exist until 1966. Even with that Decision, counsel was not automatically entitled by persons accused of all crimes. Misdemeanors or lesser crimes were not included in the Decision.

Interestingly, our history reveals that unless the Supreme Court ruled otherwise, people and citizens in this country did not have an absolute right to represent themselves. They had to have a lawyer in some capacity. These historical developments, conflicts, and confusions continued to evolve, and are still doing so today.

Now, in the United States, persons charged with any criminal act are entitled to have a lawyer represent them and, if they cannot afford it, to have one appointed by the Court. This is what created Public Defenders. Again, remember, this didn't happen until the late 60's.

As the evolution continued, and lawyers were being appointed in every type of criminal case, the competition for business among lawyers was ignited and began to burn. Before there were interpretations of the "right to counsel" our citizens had a right to acquire their own lawyers, assuming they could afford to do so. At the same time, a system of regulations began to grow rapidly in the various state lawyer Bar Associations.

In Florida, as an example, the Bar Association controlled what lawyers could do in all kinds of representations to the point of dictating what fees they were allowed to charge. In Florida we had what was known as fee schedules.

The Bar Association published regulations determining how much a lawyer could charge and be paid for different activities. The maximum that a lawyer could charge, for example, for a divorce case was $150.00. For felony criminal trials, they could charge up to $500.00. This continued to evolve as the practice of law moved from being an honorable goal and "profession" into being a business.

Along with the awareness of practicing law being a "business" came the evolution in the rules of not only the amount that could be charged, but what type of recognition or advertising a lawyer would be entitled to use. It is hard to imagine that as recently as the 60's and early 70's lawyers were not allowed to advertise in any capacity.

There were of course none of the currently repetitive, sometimes completely obnoxious, television advertisements. There were no advertisements allowed in the telephone Yellow Pages or any other publications.

As the expansion of lawyer "rights" to advertise and ultimately avoid fee schedules by charging whatever the lawyer desired in rendering his/her services in the profession, the entire system changed.

Of course, along with this concept of "business advertisement" came the recognition and use of news media to support lawyers' claims and entitlements. This evolved over the years into what it is today and is unlikely to stop or return to what was considered normal in the past. We are all aware of the persistent obnoxious television ads with exaggerated claims of experiences, qualifications, and extravagant financial results, but it has also spread into political involvements.

As recently as the early 70's, there were no cameras, still or television, allowed in courtrooms. Any news publications or efforts to spread the information came from the use of courtroom artists with their drawings and sketches.

Reporters, like other citizens, could sit in virtually all proceedings in court and then go outside and report, either by publishing articles in periodicals or having interviews. The journalistic world has embodied and appears to believe in virtually only the "First Amendment" of the United States Constitution. Those interpretations have resulted in news journalists having access to almost all judicial proceedings, although there are still some certain limitations.

Even today with the notoriety created because of all other publication sources, television cameras are not allowed in Federal courts. There does not appear to be any rational justification for separating public access under the "First Amendment" between state proceedings and Federal proceedings.

Moreover, it is worth observing that there are no established licensing or training requirements for a person to be a "journalist" and therefore have the virtually unfettered utilization and access to First Amendment Rights.

Beauticians, Morticians, Tattoo artists and barber shop "professionals" all must have licenses; every form of medical involvement requires licenses; virtually every commercial business in our country requires licenses; but not the news media. They have no qualifications, no educational minimums, and no licenses required.

This current situation regarding access to court proceedings and business activities of the lawyers and professionals has resulted in a world that would not have been recognized as recently as fifty years ago. The advertising aspect essentially began with telephone companies' use of directories and salespeople soliciting lawyers to participate in advertising, if for no other reason that "their competitors were."

Today the television advertising business is a multi-billion-dollar operation. Lawyers, regardless of qualifications and experience, can buy commercial ads in newspapers, magazines, journals, radio, and of course television. Whether they have the claimed "experiences" or not may result in some admonishments from Bar Associations, but not from journalists or any other business activities.

The result of this devolution now is epitomized by some lawyers who rush to involve themselves in any and every case they can that is possibly going to generate widespread publications and even more business.

As an example, there is no requirement that a lawyer seeking to obtain a case is publicly recognized by their profession under a supervised system of Board Certifications.

They can simply make claims as to such things as where they went to law school and how many years they have practiced. Histories of results and accomplishments are not required to be publicized.

What many people are unaware of, including many lawyers, is that it is commonplace for some of these cases to result in lawyers aggressively seeking to be involved, even though there is no monetary compensation. At least no monetary contribution for that particular case, but with assumptions that the notoriety may result in other business, and therefore the actual conduct of the defense is advertising that did not "cost" at least in dollars, anything.

With this history, it was expected and proven that when Trayvon Martin was killed in Sanford, Florida and the news media was aggressively involved in the case that there would be a line of lawyers seeking involvement and self-aggrandizement as investments in their legal future and profitability.

As has been described here and will be further discussed in this book, what happened may have questions that are never going to be absolutely answered. The bottom line is Trayvon was "Black" and was shot and killed by a neighborhood watch "commander." There was nothing noteworthy about this until it was first disclosed publicly, and the news media got hold of it.

As we will see whether it mattered or not the undisputed facts were that the victim, Trayvon, was a young Black youth in a "hoodie" who was confronted by the apparent White armed guard, and he was shot and killed. Martin was unarmed and the two people got into a confrontation. Neither knew the other and unfortunately there were no complete "eyewitnesses" that clearly saw and heard exactly what happened.

By the next day there began to be some local press coverage of the shooting, which then rocketed to first pages of news outlets throughout the country and ultimately the world. The publicity that resulted in this apparent racial confrontation grew exponentially.

Almost within hours of the first revelations there began the lawyer solicitations directly and indirectly wanting to benefit from and take advantage of the growing publicity. The shooter was not even arrested at the time and at the scene. Thus, there was a delay in the "publicity" both as to subject and degree. However, as soon as it "got out" and the media grabbed onto the apparent racial issue, there were immediate claims of lawyers to get involved.

If Mr. Zimmerman had been arrested the state would have to have presented him in court almost immediately where he would have either hired a lawyer or been asked about if he needed a lawyer to be provided for him. This didn't even happen for at least six weeks.

However, because there was some news publicity, there were some lawyers who "smelled an opportunity" and volunteered their involvement. A young lawyer unknown to the public in general, having no recognized credentials or experiences of any form of notoriety, solicited and began contacting the news media to announce his presence and purpose. In a short time, another lawyer, similarly experienced, sought the advantage of being involved in the case.

Remember there still was no case for approximately six weeks but these lawyers together and individually claimed to be the "lawyers of record" for the accused shooter, even though there was "no record." They claimed to have filed or made known their "appearance" as counsel for the shooter. That's what it's called when a lawyer files formal notices with the Court and the Prosecution that they have been retained to represent the accused. Where there is no arrest, there is no court and no formal place to "appear."

Within a matter of days of the initial story appearing in the press that there had been a shooting in Sanford, the subject matter and claim of "race" grew rapidly. Demonstrations were popping up everywhere and internationally known personalities like Reverend Al Sharpton were on the front of the line protesting the shooting and failure of arrest of the shooter.

The rampant publicity was almost unprecedented, at least for the area near Sanford, Florida. A nearby and recent circumstance regarding Casey Anthony and the death of her child was front page news everywhere.

Two lawyers who had independently "volunteered" to represent Mr. Zimmerman soon admitted that they had no contact with him, couldn't find him, and didn't know where he was.

The formal arrest, followed by the nearly unprecedented national publicity, immediately led to a new lawyer appearing in the case. The new lawyer did have qualifications as being Board Certified and was well recognized as an expert in criminal law.

However, according to all the numerous public releases and subsequent statements, this lawyer was not actually "hired" but volunteered. The shooter didn't have enough money or ability to hire a lawyer.

Not only was the case infected by repeated claims of representation, withdrawal, or denial, and ultimate determination of counsel, but there was also a series of successions of judges. Ordinarily, a crime resulting in an arrest, is followed by routine proceedings in court and a judge is assigned to handle the case.

The assigning of the judge is done randomly by the Clerk's office and computer input to those judges that are in the "criminal division." Ironically, many years ago, the judges were frequently picked by either the Clerk or sometimes lawyers pulled colored marbles out of a little box with a slot to let the marble drop and that marble was then assigned to a judge. Drawing that marble by the lawyer resulted in being assigned to that judge.

This was of course a very long time ago, before we had computers and the present process had been established. Now it is a matter of routine. There are several judges that are assigned by the Chief Judge of a Circuit to serve on a criminal bench.

In this case, the initial judge assigned was a young judge, only 39 years of age with virtually no experience in criminal cases at all. She was well-regarded and well-respected in civil matters but had been assigned after her election to the judiciary to be on the criminal bench. At the time of this series of events, she was also married to a lawyer who specialized in civil law matters. He in turn was associated with another lawyer who, despite the total lack of any meaningful credentials or certifications and reputation, was a CNN commentator or news analyst.

Because of the certain impending notoriety and high-profile coverage of this case, this judge correctly anticipated the potential conflict of her handling the case that her husband's partner would be commenting on. She was requested to remove herself from the case by the lawyer that wound up handling the case, Mr. Mark O'Mara.

Immediately upon this first judge properly removing herself from the case, the system appointed a judge who was in fact historically a criminal defense lawyer who had worked in that capacity for a significant time before becoming a judge. This judge, John Galluzzo, handled many murder cases and had been assigned criminal cases in this jurisdiction.

While Judge Galluzzo was available and appropriately experienced, he did not wind up with the case. The next judge appointed was Kenneth Lester. He was known as a high-profile veteran of cases and had significant experience in handling criminal cases, particularly major cases that were potentially death penalty cases. Another judge that was being potentially assigned to the case was Debra Nelson, who later became the trial judge after the succession of removals. Judge Nelson became the Chief Judge who would conduct the trial.

A routine bond hearing was set to determine what conditions there would be for Mr. Zimmerman to be released from custody pending his trial. In the bond hearing when evidence was presented it turned out that defendant Zimmerman and his wife had failed to reveal the existence of money that they had and basically lied in court about it.

According to reports of what happened in the hearing, evidence was presented that the defendant Zimmerman and his wife had essentially conspired to conceal assets so that he would appear indigent, thus unable to hire his own counsel. Moreover, that he would not have the money to flee the jurisdiction and violate the conditions of release or bond. Ironically this resulted in the beginning of efforts to raise money for the defendant's case that had originally been publicized as being done pro bono.

Judge Lester was very unhappy about these misrepresentations and wanted Mr. Zimmerman to be put in jail. Judge Lester had entered an Order making statements in essence revealing Mr. Zimmerman as being a manipulator that was hiding money and keeping a secret passport. These "findings" and statements by the judge resulted in defense counsel filing Motions to disqualify him. The judge refused, and he became the second judge disqualified.

The Appellate Court entered a ruling requiring Judge Lester to be replaced and the case then was assigned to Judge Nelson who had originally been directing assignments to the first judges. The process now resulted in what would be indeed the last judge to handle the case and taking it through trial.

After the succession of volunteer lawyers and changes of judges, the "cast of characters" seemed to be settled. Within a few days of the arrest that was finally made, defense attorney Mark O'Mara volunteered for the defense and became lead counsel for Mr. Zimmerman.

Based on prior representations and comments from lawyers not associated with the case, it was suggested that Mr. O'Mara should avoid attempting to try the case in the public media. Almost immediately after Mr. O'Mara formally announced his presence as counsel for Zimmerman, he conducted an interview outside his office. He had previously made a proposal to the Orange County (Orlando) Bar Association to restrict and limit public analysis made by lawyers in high profile cases. He was presenting that position to the public based upon the Casey Anthony case that was prominent in the news immediately preceding this one. In fact, he was involved in continuing press conferences of various degrees from that point forward.

At the beginning of the representation by Mr. O'Mara, a former prosecutor and judge had commented that based on his experiences with attorney O'Mara he knew that O'Mara would not attempt to try the case in the media despite his initial press conference held at his office.

In fact, and to the contrary, the defense counsel began a process of continuing almost relentless press conferences. He conducted so many that despite his own protestations it appeared that he was indeed trying the case in the press.

His repeated conferences resulted in unprecedented legal action brought by the prosecution. They filed a request for the Court to enter a Gag Order—which is a legal order that restricts the release of information to the public—to prevent counsel O'Mara from continuing to have these repeated press conferences.

The reason for seeking the "Gag Order" appears to have been appropriate. The State was concerned that the daily bombarding of defense theories and arguments related in the press would make it very difficult to select a jury. Eventually, however, the Court denied that Motion.

Predictably, upon the denial, the bombardment of defense counsel's press "releases" continued. In fact, the prosecutors tried at least three times to get Gag Orders entered by asking the judge to force Mr. O'Mara to remain quiet. It was revealed in this process that the Defense was using social media to allegedly control and filter comments about the case. There was a reported article about this issue revealing that the Defense was using Twitter, Facebook, and its own website to reinforce their side of the story.

Whether or not this actually happened is unknown to this author. However, there had been an assertion made earlier that during the infamous Casey Anthony case the Defense had "hired a team of six people to read and analyze more than forty thousand opinions on Twitter, Facebook, and various blogs and used them to craft their strategy."

This is another complete media falsehood. Your author, Cheney Mason, was senior defense counsel for Casey Anthony and has no knowledge whatsoever of any team of people reviewing social media, never heard of it, didn't do it, and sure didn't rely on any such things for anything to do with crafting a strategy.

Apparently, this is just another example of how the unprofessional media can be completely wrong but, more importantly, what lawyers now do, which is foreign to long-term established professional Code of Conduct endorsed by the Florida Bar Association.

Contrary to the initial positions attributed to defense counsel, the Defense did aggressively seek contributions of money to a fund to defend Mr. Zimmerman. A website was established that quickly raised over $200,000.00 for the "volunteer defense." The Defense presented assertions that Mr. Zimmerman had been treated "unfairly" and that he needed support because he had been accused of being a racist and was allegedly innocent of this shooting.

Not only was the original "representation" made to the public that the case would be tried in court and not the media, but it was also represented that it was being done without fee. That purportedly based on the assertion that defense counsel felt that the defendant Zimmerman had been and was being mistreated and needed funds for a legal defense.

In reality, Mr. Zimmerman and his attorneys had been soliciting donations for his defense since their initial involvement with the case, and they had purportedly raised over $400,000.00.

An additional conflict arose when a well-known civil rights lawyer, Benjamin Crump, made his appearance in the entire scenario as counsel representing the family of the deceased victim, Trayvon Martin. Mr. Crump has a well-known history, repeated in this case, of making public appearances and assertions on behalf of victims or alleged victims of civil rights violations.

The Defense argued that because of public appearances by the victim's family, it was appropriate for the Defendant to have balance in revelations for the public. Predictably, the various news media opposed any Gag Orders.

An interesting theory arising from this case has revealed some important concerns about the actions of the lawyers for the Prosecution. Looking at the trial from an historical perspective, the Prosecution did not seem to be as aggressive as they could have been in presenting the case.

In fact, even in the closing of the trial the lead Prosecutor in his closing conceded that he did not know what had happened. He offered conflicting possibilities as to what had happened leading up to the shooting. That type of approach established unequivocally a "reasonable doubt" that by itself almost assured an acquittal of Mr. Zimmerman.

During the reporting on the case the press consulted a number of local lawyers. Some who had no relevant history or experience in the area but rendered all kinds of opinions. There was no shortage of volunteer "consultants" for the news media. Some of these so-called consultants had no qualifications or experience that would justify any valid public comments.

Unfortunately, this type of scenario has become all too common. Some lawyers so desperate for publicity volunteer repeatedly to comment on what they were thinking at the time and not necessarily based on any real evidence.

Chapter Eleven

JURY SELECTION

In our country, persons accused of crimes are generally entitled to a determination of their guilt or innocence by having a jury trial. That has been basically the essence of our "system of justice" since the creation of our country and constitution. However, there have been exceptions to this system not known or recognized by the general public. Among those exceptions were situations where the ability of the state to present jury trials was non-existent.

In the 1970s, municipal courts in Florida normally did not have the facilities or personnel and thus the capability to provide jury trials. If a Defendant was arrested in a small municipality and charged with misdemeanor offenses such as DUI, while they were technically entitled to a jury trial, they could not get one in that municipality.

Accordingly, back in those days defense lawyers frequently would just file a motion to demand a jury trial, knowing that the municipal court of that jurisdiction could not provide such. As a result, the case would automatically be dismissed. After several years of this practice, the municipal courts were consolidated within the county courts and that approach was no longer viable.

It seems hard to imagine in these days, but in fact we went through long periods of our history with "exceptions" to the right to a jury trial. Even where there were physical abilities to provide the needed infrastructure, there were many occasions where judges would make initial agreements with prosecution and defense counsel that, if the defendant would admit to being guilty, there would be no jail time if they would waive a jury trial.

This was frequently done and then this too disappeared. Now, these various "exceptions" have effectively been abolished and under the accepted and uniform rules of criminal procedure in Florida, a defendant charged with a crime can always have a jury trial, if they want one.

The singularly most important aspect of the conduct of a "jury trial" is the selection of the actual jury. This may seem fundamental but in fact it is a subject that requires a great deal of learning and experience to have meaningful effect. The process of establishing a jury is referred to as Voir Dire, meaning to speak the truth. When defendants are facing a jury trial, they have a right to either represent themselves or have legal counsel do it.

The next question is how does someone become or avoid becoming a juror? Some people have a desire to be a member of a jury, while many people look for excuses to avoid that obligation and civic duty for reasons of their own. Thus, we go through a process known as jury selection where the lawyers for both sides are, within certain restrictions, allowed to ask questions of prospective jurors. This is done in an effort to determine not just the qualifications, but whether they, the lawyers, feel they may have some "advantage" for their side of the case depending on who those jurors are.

For a very long period potential jurors were summoned to the courthouse by the Clerk of Court. The Clerk simply reviewed their records of registered voters and sent notices (allegedly randomly) to those voters summoning them to come to the courthouse on such and such a date for potential jury duty.

This approach created the ability to seek advantage for one side or the other based on political affiliation and was eventually determined to be inappropriate. The law was then changed to use driver's license registrations, since they did not reveal any potential political bias.

Of course, anybody receiving a summons to appear for jury duty had the right to either accept that obligation as a citizenship entitlement, or for numerous reasons to reject it. We now have at least a list of specific excuses that can automatically avoid the obligation.

Inherently within the laws of Florida, there are people who are automatically disqualified or automatically given an excuse option if they want it. Convicted felons are not qualified to be jurors; persons over the age of 70 are allowed to opt out if they want to, similarly persons with certain disabilities may be voluntarily dismissed.

A question that has frequently been raised in various circumstances is why or how did the jury in this case wind up being six women? Additionally, they have been described as six White women. There are required Constitutional observations as to classes or categories of prospective jurors—no such objections, motions, or issues were raised in this case.

The ordinary process in picking a jury is essentially one with elimination. Questions during the Voir Dire establish qualifications, but they also give suggestions to the trial lawyers of things to be avoided. We can only conclude that in this circumstance these jurors were "what was left." Nothing magic about it; it just simply is the circumstances that resulted after the various peremptory and/or causal challenges were made. There could be no question that both sides, the Prosecution and Defense, agreed to accept the makeup of this jury.

The process generally begins by assembling those persons who have been summoned and have not sought automatic excuses. The judge will ordinarily start the process by reading the Indictment or Information accusing the defendant of whatever criminal offense is at issue. The judge will also generally go through the automatic potential excuses that summoned citizens can use to avoid their duty.

After that is done, there is then questioning of the prospective jurors by the lawyers. In Federal Court, the judges do the questioning and, in most circumstances, only allow the lawyers to have very limited questions. Most often this is done by submitting proposed questions in writing to the Court who will then decide whether they will allow the specific question to be used.

This has proven historically to be very conflicting. It depends on the objectivity, experience, and often basic intelligence of the judge. Given the fact that we have such limited requirements for a person to qualify as a judge, this makes this a very artful process rather than a predictable or established one.

The question frequently raised is where the judges come from? Who are they, and how do they become judges?

Federal judges are appointed for life by the politicians in charge of the government at the time. There are very few formal requirements for this type of judicial appointment; only that he or she is a lawyer, citizen, and not a convicted felon.

In Florida state courts, all that is required is that the prospective judge be a member of the Florida Bar and, depending on what the level of judge they are being considered for, a determination of how many years they have been lawyers admitted to the Bar. Some are well qualified after only a few years of experience as a lawyer; others, no matter how many years they have been members of the Bar, are not or should never be qualified to play this key role in our judicial system.

The Constitution of the State of Florida, Article IV, is the creation of the executive branch of the government. It begins with the creation of the office of Governor and establishing qualifications for the office. To be a Governor of the State of Florida, the person must have resided in the state for the preceding seven years and be at least thirty years of age. There is no other requirement with respect to education, experience, or any forms of history.

Within the concept of creating the executive branch, we also have, in the Constitution, Article V, entitled "The Judiciary." Pursuant to the Constitution, we create a Supreme Court, Appellate Court Districts, and Judicial Circuits following county lines. In order to become a member of the Supreme Court, one must have been a member of the Florida Bar Association for at least the preceding ten years of the appointment. To be eligible for appointment as a Circuit Judge, the candidate must have been a member of the Florida Bar for the preceding five years. That same requirement applies to candidates to become county court judges.

It may be interesting to understand that there are really no other required qualifications. While we have, in Florida, and for the last approximate forty years, recognized established areas of law for consideration and entitlement as Board Certified. We initially created Board Certification for civil trial lawyers and thereafter criminal trial lawyers, family lawyers, general contracts, construction, aviation, and others. Each of these specialty qualifications required substantial experience in those areas of law, as well as peer review by other lawyers and judges, and passing special examinations.

Unfortunately, there are no such requirements for anyone to be considered as a judge, be it County judge, Circuit judge, District Appeal Court judge, or Supreme Court judge. In recent history, the Governor of the state of Florida, despite being a lawyer himself and therefore charged with certain knowledge, made an appointment to the Florida Supreme Court of a completely unqualified person. Remember, the only qualifications by our Constitution are that a candidate for the Supreme Court must have been a member of the Florida Bar for the preceding ten years. Governor DeSantis, choosing to ignore the law, or otherwise potentially just being ignorant of it, appointed a lawyer to serve on the Supreme Court that by Constitutional Law was not qualified. When it was pointed out to the Governor that this candidate had not been a member of the Florida Bar for at least the preceding ten years, his retort was, "well once she's appointed, after a period of time, she will meet the ten-year qualification." It may be challenging to the imagination to expect that a person, claiming to be a lawyer under the same Constitution elected to be Governor, could so flagrantly ignore the law as to make an illegal appointment knowingly and voluntarily. Equally, the candidate wanting to be on the Supreme Court knew, or had to have known, herself that she wasn't qualified to even apply, much less accept the appointment. That lawsuit was filed and without surprise the existing unanimous Supreme Court (including majority appointed by the Governor) ruled that the appointment of this non-ten-year qualified candidate was in violation of the Constitution, and she could not be a member of the Supreme Court. Not to be surprised, the Governor waited until the time had passed and this candidate met the ten-year requirement so that on the next vacancy, he reappointed her.

Historically, one of the concerns has been that with the advent of the law requiring such intense knowledge, especially in matters dealing with family law and criminal law, it would seem that a person set to adjudicate those issues would have to be Board Certified. Despite having the Board Certification program for lawyers there is still no requirement that any judicial candidate must be qualified within the field of law.

More perplexing is that under the Judiciary Article V, a Chief Judge, as elected by the contemporary members of the Circuit, appoints, and designates the duties of the other judges.

The Chief Judge appoints the judges handling all cases, including divorce cases, criminal cases, personal injury, and contract cases. We have unfortunately experienced numerous situations where a Chief Judge appoints a new member, or changes the duties of the others, to make judicial decisions and rule in cases in which they have absolutely no experience whatsoever. There have been judges that obtain that title with no court experience at all. There have been judges whose only experience as lawyers was personal injury accident cases who became judges and were then placed in charge of criminal law sections to determine such matters as Death Penalty cases. It is also worth noting that judges are required to be judges full time. They are not allowed to engage in the practice of law or hold office in any political party.

Judges are also subject to election once they have obtained office. Contrary to most popular belief, the persons seeking to become judge don't just run for office and become judges by public election. Most often, judges become judges by appointment of the Governor. When the determined term as set forth by the Judicial Nominating Committee is concluded, they then run for election or retention.

During elections, the general population does not usually cast their votes for judges. A significant percentage of citizens who go through the trouble to attend the poles and cast ballots do not know who the judges are, don't know or care about their performance, are simply tired of going down the list (from President on down) and do not bother to vote for the bottom of the ballot, which is where the judicial candidates are listed. Historically, votes for those positions constitute around twenty percent of the total of people that showed up and voted.

Additionally, Supreme Court judges and District Court judges whose terms, as established by the Constitution, are ending are then eligible for re-election on a basis of "merit retention." That is that the normal election ballot simply has the name of the Court and one question for the voters: Shall justice X (name of the judge and name of the Court) be retained in office? It requires only a majority of the electors to determine the retention as a yes or a no. This process has been going on in Florida now for many years, yet not a single judge subject to retention has ever been removed by a majority vote answering "no." In fact, there haven't even been any close yes versus no decisions. In the event that some judge or justice suffers a majority "no" vote as retention, then at the end of that term the Governor appoints a replacement.

The concern about the qualifications of judiciary in this history should be in the forefront of all citizens. When we as citizens are being faced with what are now frequently called "high profile" cases, we have a right and should be able to rely on qualified judges. Remember, there are no qualifications to be a judge sitting on these cases. As a rule, those who may be assigned to adjudicate Death Penalty cases would require additional qualifications. That is extremely rare.

In the case of Trayvon Martin, as we have seen, there were several judges that were in and out of being the assigned judge to the case. While there were no qualifications other than being a judge, there also were no requirements for any special training or experience because it was not a Death Penalty case. The judge who handled this case did have experience and was qualified fully within those qualifications as exhibited by our Constitution.

What most Board-Certified lawyers know is that the process of selecting the jury is both scientific and artful. Cases are almost always won or lost during the process of selecting the jury. Experienced lawyers know that they can essentially "try" the case in the process of questioning prospective jurors. Sometimes the process is done in a very short time, a few hours, other occasions result in days or weeks of questioning prospective jurors before they are deemed "qualified" and selected to serve on the jury.

There are enumerable subjects that can be discussed in the "questioning." Commonly the lawyers are aware of this and frequently attempt to "try the case" in the process, running into objections by the opposing side or sometimes the judges.

Experienced lawyers know that many judges start the process from a viewpoint of prejudice. Some are better at hiding it than others, but it is overwhelmingly clear that by the time a trial starts, based on the history of pretrial motions and hearings, judges, obligated to be open-minded and objective, often are not.

There are no specific limitations enumerated as to what matters can be asked of prospective jurors and which are prohibited. Even when there are such apparent distinctions, they are frequently arguable and depending on the individual personalities of the lawyers and judge involved in the case.

The process of going through the jury questioning and selection is usually unique to the case: the charges brought, the notoriety, if any, and the personalities involved.

Obviously before the jury selection process begins, the lawyers involved must have a good understanding of what the facts are in the case. They should know everything about the case that is beneficial to their side and those issues that are damning to their side. The lawyers need to be able to present themselves to the jurors as if they are in fact on trial. To a certain extent, they are.

If the jury does not like the lawyer's presentations by attitude, language, or body language, that lawyer is already in trouble. This does not mean that just because a lawyer may be entertaining and presentable to the jury that they necessarily have an advantage. It is, however, a real issue and as your author believes, is present in every jury trial.

Prospective jurors need to be comfortable and accept their burden. There is no limit to the issues that could and should be discussed with them, but certainly what matters to them needs to be discovered to the best of the lawyers' ability. If a case is high profile and a juror does not want to be a member of the decision-making process they may try to get out of the responsibility. Assuming that they have already been denied their overall "excuses" unsuccessfully presented to a judge, they may still have others.

Accordingly, it is universally important in high profile cases that the jurors be informed that they can meet their civic responsibility with protected anonymity. They are questioned as an assigned number rather than their name. Of course, the judge, court personnel, and the lawyers from both sides know the names of the prospective jurors and in varying degrees information about their residency, education, employment, prior services, and other relevant information readily available on the internet.

The public, if there are television cameras involved, don't see the face of the jurors unless they are in the actual courtroom watching. Even then they don't know their names or addresses. Prospective jurors in such cases are told by the Court from the beginning, in those cases that are televised, that their faces, names, and identifying characteristics are not revealed to the public.

Federal Courts, for not necessarily acceptable reasons in these times, do not allow cameras in the courtrooms to film or disclose what happens. There have been efforts to try to "cure" that problem for many decades, without success even as of this date. However most state courts, and clearly in Florida, do allow cameras to record the entire court proceedings, except the faces and identities of the jurors.

Debate about the value of cameras in the courtroom will likely carry on for years or decades to come. What I do know, based on my over fifty years of experience and more than three hundred and fifty jury trials, the cameras do have an impact on the conduct of the court proceedings.

Jurors, even after being clearly informed that they will not be seen by the public, still almost always modify their appearances. They come to court after being selected by wearing their "Sunday best" as we used to say. Judges frequently change their appearances and attitudes and even sometimes have makeovers because they know they are being televised and presented live to their constituents, the people who will elect them to their jobs in the state courts when their terms expire.

Jurors at this level of trial, as in virtually all Florida state jury trials, fill out questionnaires that are distributed to the court personnel and lawyers well prior to the selection process. The addresses and thus location of residency is revealed.

There is no question that there are areas of residency that are more likely areas generally affiliated with one political philosophy, or another based on life experiences. Lawyers should not only know about the area in which they are having a trial but from the questionnaires the historical residencies of probable jurors.

There is no exact science to this, but it is very clear that some neighborhoods, as example, may be overwhelmingly wealthy White and therefore probably Republican areas. While other neighborhoods are overwhelmingly Black or minorities, and therefore more likely liberal and anti-law enforcement.

Both conclusions are subject to possible immediate and valid challenges. It is something that competent lawyers will know.

Whether it is Republican, Democrat, Black, White, or another minority, the outcome is not absolute in every circumstance. Along with other things, it should be something that an experienced lawyer is aware of and will be part of private considerations.

Prior service as a juror can be very revealing. Most people will not have prior service because the odds of being selected are narrow. However, there usually are at least one or two prospective jurors that have previously been on juries. That should alert the lawyer that this prospective juror has been, in the past, acceptable for that role.

Accordingly, those who acknowledge prior service are properly subjected to inquiry as to when, what court, what type of case, criminal or civil they served on. If criminal, the nature of the charge, and properly whether they reached a verdict. It should be pointed out that the actual verdict reached is generally not allowed to be inquired about.

In questioning the jurors in criminal cases, some of the questions presented would not only deal with that juror's history, but what history, if any they have with members of their family. Do they have family members who are prior defendants or victims? Depending on the answer, the questioner is justified in pursuing more details.

Similarly, depending on the nature of the case to be tried, it is appropriate to make certain that the jurors are aware of what the possible penalties could be before they are called upon to make a decision. In murder cases, or others facing potential death sentences, it is mandatory for the prospective jurors to be what is referred to as "death qualified."

A prospective juror that reveals he or she could in proper circumstances impose a death penalty, that response makes them basically qualified. If a prospective juror reveals that they could not impose the death penalty, they are automatically disqualified.

As suggested earlier, people being potentially selected have an opportunity to seek to either avoid or delay their "service" depending on the facts. Sometimes people have work obligations, and they may be influenced by the estimated time required for the trial. In other words, they may be able to devote one or two days to the process, but if they are advised that the trial may last several weeks that almost always provides a potential and significant hardship that would disqualify jurors.

In this same vein, there are many cases that due to the publicity and nature of the case, may require the jurors to be sequestered. That means that if they are selected, they are sent home or taken home by law enforcement to get what they will need, including their medicine and clothes then taken back to be housed in a hotel or similar for the duration of the trial. They are not allowed to watch uncensored news. They are not allowed to have conversations with family or friends at all about the trial. They are not even allowed to talk among themselves about the trial prior to determinations to be made by actual deliberations as a "whole jury."

Appropriate questioning is essential to learn what the jurors know or "think they know" about the case before it even is presented to them. High publicity cases such as this one involving the killing of Trayvon Martin occupied all sources of media coverage (as can be seen in the attached Bibliography).

Sometimes the news reports are accurate; unfortunately, as we all know many times the so-called "journalists" have exaggerated, misrepresented, or just simply been wrong as to what happened. That is why sequestered jurors are not allowed to be exposed to the "media" reports. In many situations, certainly those with high profile publicity, the prospective juror may have, well in advance of even being summoned as a prospective juror, had discussions with family or friends about the case.

It is also common that prospective jurors are members of various organizations or clubs. Some of them are notorious for espousing prejudices, philosophies, or controlling politics that would affect the trial they are being considered for.

An additional issue about jury selection is that we have continually evolving laws of what qualifications must be. For decades, even after voting rights legislation was passed in the sixties, we have had jurors selected considering substantial reliance on issues of race, gender, religion, and sexual orientation. One by one the Courts have determined the Constitutional issues about that. It is inappropriate and not allowed for jurors to be excused, or sought to excuse, solely based on any of these issues.

Generally, jurors are questioned by lawyers representing both sides. The lawyers are entitled to make objections, known as "challenges" and arguments for or against prospective jurors being allowed to serve. There are rules that determine how many challenges a lawyer is entitled to. These types of challenges are referred to as peremptory challenges. This means that the lawyer can tell the court that they don't want a particular juror to be on the jury simply because they don't like something about them.

Depending on the nature of the charge, a number of such challenges are allowed. The lawyer challenging a person must be able to intelligently explain to the court why they don't want that juror. This is especially true when the prospective juror is a recognized "minority" based on race, religion, sex, or some other clearly involved issue.

Accordingly, the "peremptory" right to excuse a juror is not absolute. However, there are what are known as "causal challenges." Usually, a person who is subject to being excluded because of "cause" has said or done something that is not acceptable to both sides and the court.

When the jury selection process is completed, the lawyer must be ready to start to try the case. For the lawyers it is mandatory to know the facts that have been developed, as well as understand the theory of both the prosecution and the defense.

In this case it was clear that there were really two people involved: the defendant Mr. Zimmerman on trial for the charge of Second-Degree Murder, and the victim, Trayvon Martin.

The Prosecution is required to present the evidence in accordance with the rules and laws of criminal proceedings. The Prosecution always gets to go first in the jury selection. Thus, a competent prosecutor acting in good faith and believing the guilt of the accused, should know the evidence extremely well and present it to the jurors during the selection process in the form of questions.

In this case, the Prosecution had the advantage of knowing the defense strategy that had actually been previously presented by the Defendant. Recall that the day after the actual killing of Trayvon Martin the Defendant was allowed, and even accompanied by Sheriff's Deputies, to create a reenactment of the crime.

This was not something that the Defendant was required to do or could have been made to do. It was something he wanted to do. His lawyers were not involved and were smart enough to quietly avoid commenting on the process.

Accordingly, the prosecution knew that the defense was claiming that he reacted in self-defense because he "feared for his life" at the hands of young Trayvon. The Defendant claimed that Trayvon had knocked him down and was bashing his head against the side-walk. The Defendant claimed that the severe injuries he sustained caused him to believe that he was going to be killed and needed to defend himself.

The prosecution then should have asked prospective jurors what, if any experience, they had ever had with head wounds or falling on sidewalks—getting injured and the like. They did not do so. Likewise, the prosecution could have, had they the evidence, questioned jurors about any knowledge they had about DNA.

In addition, for questions about potential injuries, knowing the likely and intended presentations by the defense, they could have asked numerous questions of the jurors to reveal their impressions of the case. Have any of you ever experienced a situation where someone has inflicted an injury on themselves in an effort to appear sympathetic or victimized by somebody else?

Given the apparent lack of argument as to when and where this killing occurred, the appropriate questions of prospective jurors should include what experience any of them had with either being a security guard, having friends or relatives who worked as security guards, or have they ever been subjected to actions by security guards.

Obviously, anyone who had prior personal experience as a security guard, or had other relationships with them, would and should be exposed to questions for their potential bias or prejudice. They were not.

The prosecution could have and should have asked questions of potential jurors related to having personally experienced someone lying to or about them. Similarly, they should explore discussions they may have had where someone they were dealing with frequently changed their story.

The prosecution knew or should have known the publicly reported numbers of times that the shooter had changed his story and used false allegations to justify his shooting of Trayvon. Proper questions of this subject would in essence have been telling the jury what the trial was going to be about, and therefore whether they were "qualified" to sit in judgment.

The evidence in this case was such that the defense Board-Certified lawyers knew to ask questions that would lead to justifying Mr. Zimmerman's actions.

The defense in this case was totally accurate in forecasting the future. They knew that the prosecution was going to present to the jury the entire video recording of the Defendant's next day reenactment. They knew that by the prosecution doing that they were relying on it as admission tantamount to a confession.

However, the Prosecution obviously underestimated the reality that such "reenactment" was establishing an important strategy for the defense. The lawyers for the Defendant also knew that, thanks to the State Prosecutors errors, they would not have to put their client on the stand to testify and thereby be cross-examined.

Most experienced defense lawyers do not ever really consider putting their client on the stand to testify. If you know the evidence well enough there are other methods of presenting defensive positions if nothing other than argument on "facts" that had not been prematurely discussed or presented by the prosecution.

It is considered factual that defendants who do not testify have a much higher likelihood of acquittal than those who do take the stand and suffer cross-examination. Unless they have absolute defenses such as unimpeachable alibis or other independent witnesses justifying their actions, they simply do not testify. Remember the burden of proving every element of the alleged crime and proof to the exclusion of all reasonable doubt is a burden on the prosecution.

The defense normally has no burden of proof in the trial. If the defense had succumbed to the enticement to present the reenactment themselves by a Motion for Defense on "Stand Your Ground", as has been discussed, the Defendant would have been vigorously cross-examined and undoubtedly the results could have been entirely different.

A very important line of questioning of jurors should attempt to learn the actual "exposure" or awareness that a prospective juror may have about the case. The prospective juror should be asked such things as "How do you get your news?" "Do you read newspapers?" "Do you watch television?" "Is there any particular journalist or media person that you frequently listen to or observe?" As example, there are some so-called "journalists" who historically have been shown to be clearly prejudiced and bias. They can use their public platform position to espouse their theories of the defendant's guilt or innocence.

A good example could be cited in the case of Casey Anthony. The former Attorney General of the State of Florida and recently confirmed Attorney General for the United States, Ms. Pam Bondi, made public pronouncements during the Casey Anthony case (which she had nothing to do with) that she believed Ms. Anthony was guilty. She stated that she would help ensure that Ms. Anthony got the maximum sentence.

Despite that unprofessional and improper public statement by the then Florida Attorney General, Ms. Anthony was found not guilty. No apology or admission of being wrong was ever made by Ms. Bondi.

One of the historically proven values to lawyers in selecting the jury is what I refer to as "electing the foreman." First, don't get confused, the foreman is secretly and privately elected by the fellow members of the jury once they are all selected and embodied in the jury room.

However, during Voir Dire a lawyer may ask a prospective juror a telling question: If you were elected as foreperson of this jury, would you be willing to accept that responsibility? It is not unusual for a prospective juror to equivocate on that answer. What is important is not just the answer, but the way human nature comes into play in this situation.

Most of us have had some experience of being in various groups or organizations, in business, politics, or social activities. Every organization needs a leader, a president, manager, or chairperson. Usually, when I have asked such a question it apparently carries on to the jury room. A person being mentioned as potential "foreman" is almost always then reaffirmed as such by the rest of the jurors when they start the case. "Electing" a "foreman" in this fashion is usually very beneficial to the side of the case which asked the question.

Chapter Twelve

THE TRIAL

The single gunshot was fired at around 7:30 pm. on the evening of February 26, 2011. There was no dispute as to who fired the shot and the results. Seventeen-year-old Trayvon Martin was killed by that gunshot. The shooter, George Zimmerman, did not physically try to flee.

He had been recorded calling the police department in Sanford, Florida advising that he was following a "suspicious suspect." He was instructed by the police not to follow and that police were on the way. The police arrived a minute and a half after the shot was fired. Immediately, it was clear to all concerned that this young man was dead from a gunshot wound to his chest. He was unarmed, possessing nothing on his person other than a can of iced tea, some Skittles, his phone, $40.15, a red lighter, headphones and a photo pin.

There were some "witnesses" who heard various sounds and had seen some of what had transpired. There was no formal accusation about the shooting for some six weeks. Ordinarily and without any recorded exception, a formal arrest of Mr. Zimmerman should have been made right then at the time of the shooting.

In reality, it took public reaction, including hundreds of demonstrations and protests by ordinary citizens and celebrities nationwide before anything was done. There was no arrest or accusation made against the man who had shot and killed this unarmed teenager. The protests and outrage went all the way to the President of the United States. It was only after the outcry was so loud that formal charges and arrest of the shooter was made after approximately four months of national anger and protest.

After approximately sixteen months, a trial was ready to commence. Finally, a "jury of his peers" was selected to determine the legal guilt or innocence of the shooter. A jury of six white women was chosen.

The Constitution of the United States, as well as the state of Florida and every-where in our country, provides that an accused person is entitled to be tried by a "jury of their peers." This has been an elusive concept discussed in various circumstances and approaches since it was created. Having practiced criminal law for over fifty years, your co-author cannot define what is meant by "peer."

The accused in this case, shooter George Zimmerman, is essentially a White male with some Hispanic ancestry; he is not a doctor or a lawyer, professional athlete, celebrity, or anything identifying him in a way that would put him in a category to be considered "peered."

The victim, Trayvon Martin, was a young (seventeen-year-old) black male who was unarmed and shot and killed by Mr. Zimmerman. One can argue that the entitlement to a "jury of peers" applies only to the Defendant. That is also legally confusing and subject to much debate.

In this situation the victim, Trayvon, was accused of having provoked if not caused the entire incident. Wouldn't he be entitled to a "jury of his peers" to make those determinations?

What were the criteria for someone to be a "peer" in this case? For certain, young Trayvon was young, Black, not a professional athlete, celebrity, professionally educated person or member of any other "category" to which one might attempt to define within a category of "peers."

Despite the widespread public interest in this case which provoked nationwide and worldwide attention, the "race card" was not played. The dispute about the propriety of that fact will likely carry on as long as the memory of this case. What we know is that there were hundreds of demonstrations and protests throughout the country and other parts of the world. There was not a day without news about this case. Every television station, radio, newspaper, and other public media had multiple, if not daily news coverage about the case. There were racially oriented comments pro and con made from every strata from top to bottom of our society.

The then Governor of Florida, Rick Scott, was finally motivated to appoint a special prosecutor. Governor Scott was seen in a related televised discussion about the case wearing cowboy boots emblazoned with a Confederate Flag. While much of history relates that symbol to different aspects of the Civil War, there is no dispute that the "Confederate Flag" has become and was then symbolic of an historically racist attitude.

Jury Selection began on June 10, 2013. Potential jurors were advised that they would be sequestered and ultimately a jury was seated on June 20, 2013. There is no way that this all white, non-black, female jury was "of the peers" of the victim, who was accused of instigating the problem. Whether or not one can consider this jury in fact of being "of the peers" of Mr. Zimmerman is a matter of personal evaluation.

This case had already become a national Civil Rights cause célèbres. There were tens of thousands of protesters including nationally known leaders Reverend Al Sharpton and Reverend Jesse Jackson pouring into Sanford, Florida. According to numerous news sources, there were more than a million people who signed a Petition outraged that Zimmerman had not even been arrested for the shooting.

In a pretrial hearing, the Court ruled that it would be appropriate for the prosecution to refer to Zimmerman as a "wannabe cop" and that Trayvon Martin was profiled. However, the definition of "profiled" was left to be determined and subject to cross examination. The prosecution suggested that there were many ways that a person could be "profiled" other than just race, but that discussion was to be left for when the argument was made, and testimony presented.

One of the most fundamental requirements of any defense lawyer, even the most experienced, is that you should never under any circumstances, make an opening statement promise to the jury that they will not see or hear presented to them later in the trial. Jurors remember opening statements and will not trust the lawyer that made a promise in an opening statement that was not kept in the subsequent proceedings.

From the beginning of the trial, one of the major issues was interpretations of the recorded voice of the person screaming for help. Arguments and debates had been made with and without experts prior to trial. The issue was whether the voice heard crying for help was the shooter Zimmerman or the seventeen-year-old who was accosted and then murdered.

Experts were brought in to render opinions, as well as testimony from the deceased family and some friends of the Defendant. One of the questionable approaches in the questioning of the "hearing" witnesses was the defense counsel inappropriately being allowed to ask a witness if he had "heard anger" in the voice recorded. That conclusive testimony was allowed without objection.

One of the witnesses was a police department member who oversees Neighborhood Watch volunteers, as well as the President of the Homeowners Association where Mr. Zimmerman claimed to be watch commander. He testified that the Neighborhood Watch person was not supposed to get involved in any way, but only report to the police and then stay out of the way.

A couple of the witnesses were neighbors who lived near to where the shooting took place. The prosecution solicited testimony that included a claim that there was a fight, some muffled sounds, and that one was on top of the other. Important points that were key components of what happened varied between witnesses.

This issue occurred during the scenario when the victim, Trayvon, was on the phone talking to his girlfriend in Miami. She had testified that Martin had exclaimed concern that a "creepy ass cracker" was following him. Then there were muffled sounds. The State had a witness testify about the fight that may have been initially thought to benefit the prosecution.

However, the rest of that prosecution witness' testimony was that she heard multiple gunshots and described them as "pop, pop, pop." There is no dispute that there was only one gunshot and that was never an issue. The forensic evidence is not disputed. There was a single shot. This testimony was of no value and established one of the serious mistakes by the prosecution.

There is no excuse for the Prosecutor calling such a witness and eliciting such testimony. This raises one of the issues as to the genuine intention of the prosecution that appears in conflict with what their duty was supposed to be.

The prosecution also presented an alleged "eyewitness." This gentleman alleged to have observed part of the fight, looking out his own condominium window. He variously positioned the parties either on top or on bottom during the "fight." Ultimately, he changed his testimony to admit that he never saw anybody being grabbed and having their head slammed against the sidewalk.

Prosecution medical experts testifying at trial consisted of Dr. Shiping Bao, the pathologist who performed the autopsy on Trayvon Martin and Dr. Valerie Rao, a forensic pathologist from Jacksonville, FL.

As a very experienced and accomplished forensic pathologist, Dr. Valarie Rao was as well qualified to analyze a forensic gunshot wound case as was the defense expert. Both were considerably more able to communicate the findings to the jury than was Dr. Bao, who struggled with English as a second language, as well as having the least experience of the group. She was not questioned at all by the State regarding the gunshot injury, but only asked about the severity of the injuries to the shooter.

The majority of Dr. Bao's testimony was centered on the proximity of the wound to Martin's body and discussion of the significance of the areas of punctate thermal injuries on his skin caused by burning gunpowder. The presence of which is an indication that the gun was within approximately six inches from the skin when the bullet was fired. (Image on the next page repeated for reader convenience.)

While discussing the stippling and its significance at some length, little attention appeared to be paid to a seemingly obvious discrepancy between what is clear from the photos and Dr. Shiping Bao's description of the bullet's trajectory thru the body, that the wound tract in the left side of the chest went straight back.

For a bullet to go straight back from the chest, the end of the barrel necessarily needs to be parallel to the skin surface—with no angularity—and the burning gunpowder would create a concentric circle around the entry defect created by the bullet itself.

The photo of the entrance wound taken from the YouTube video of the testimony shows a distinctly different stippling pattern from what would be seen in the straight-on path of the bullet in Dr. Bao's description, both from the autopsy report and his testimony at trial.

113

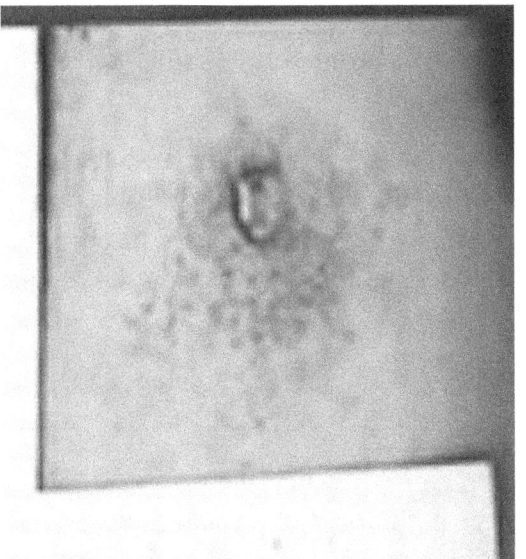

In this photo there is significantly more of the stippling pattern on the skin below the area of entry than above it where there the stippling is essentially absent. This is indicative of a gun being held at an angle, and consistent with the wound tract described in the autopsy report but not reported as such at the trial.

Judging by the stippling pattern, the bullet would have traveled left-to-right and downward, precisely what is described in the autopsy report and represented in the schematic diagram below, not straight back as Dr. Bao reported.

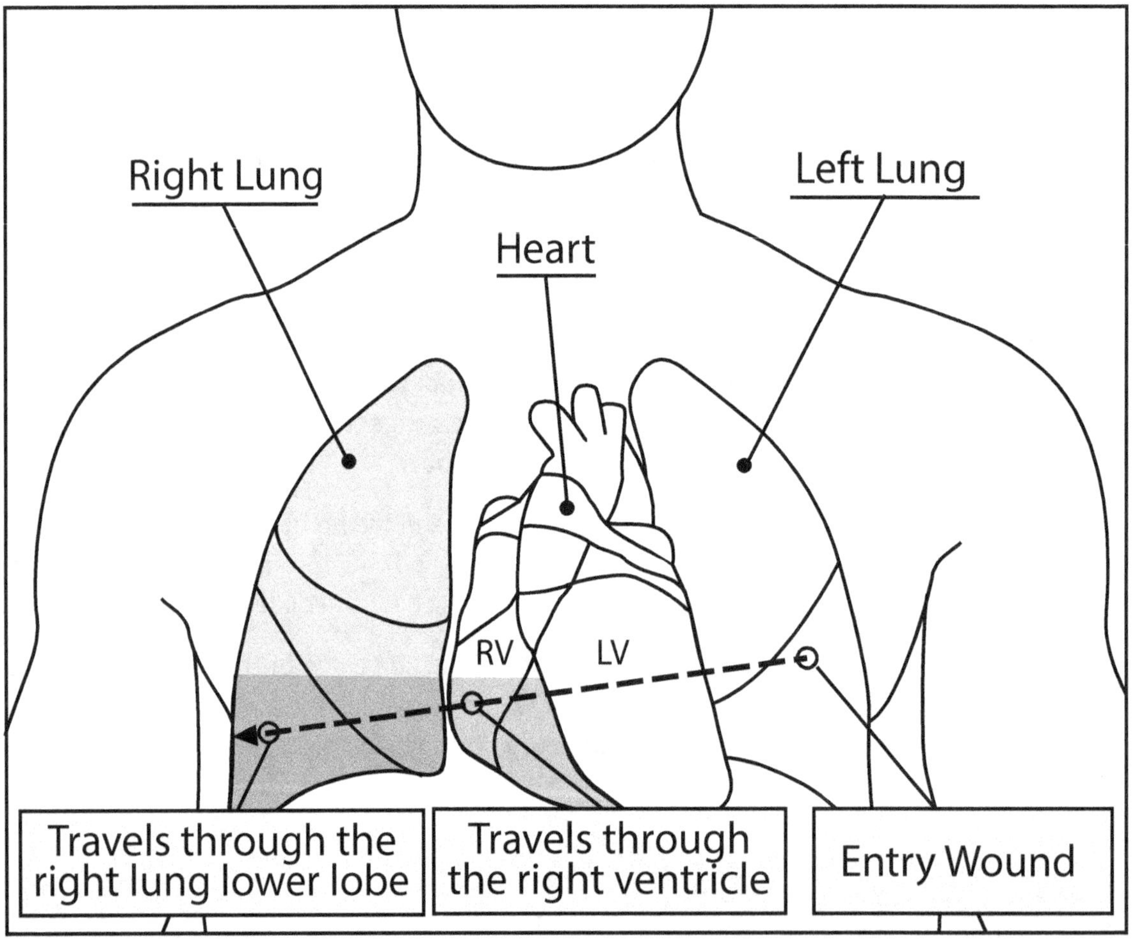

Photo showing stippling pattern as presented to the jury around the wound from the gunpowder.

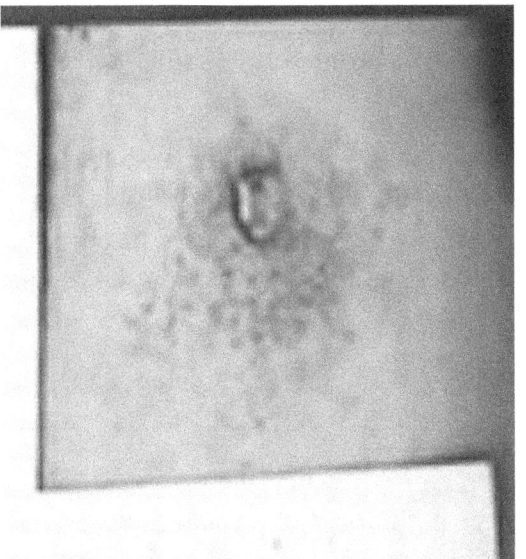

Right Lung

Left Lung

Heart

RV   LV

Travels through the right lung lower lobe

Travels through the right ventricle

Entry Wound

According to all accounts, the descriptions from Dr. Bao were accepted at face value by the State and certainly not challenged by the Defense attorneys who were most likely quite happy with staying as far away as possible from that issue.

Dr. Bao was not only somewhat inexperienced, but since English was not his primary language, he had some difficulty in presenting his findings to the jury. Later he would create a courtroom incident when after reading prepared written answers to questions from the defense, refused to allow the lawyers to see his notes until ordered to do so by the presiding Judge.

In any event, at no time in the trial was this critical error regarding the wound tract relative to the reenactment of the incident, according to the shooter addressed. It is also somewhat puzzling that Dr. Valarie Rao, a very competent and experienced forensic pathologist, who at the time was the Chief Medical Examiner for the district that included Jacksonville overlooked that. She was obviously well-known to the Jacksonville-based attorneys prosecuting the case but was not questioned at all about the gunshot wound. Rather, she only was asked to opine as to the severity, or lack thereof, of the injuries to Zimmerman's head.

The same cannot be said of the direct examination by the defense attorneys of their primary medical expert Dr. Vincent DiMaio.

According to news accounts, Dr. DiMaio indicates that "the defendant suffered at least six blows to the head and should have been taken to the hospital."

Wounds shown in photo taken in police station show three linear wounds with sharp margins located in the upper occipital scalp in the back of the head, with only a moderate amount of associated blood on the surrounding skin.

Impact of the head against a hard surface, such as a cement sidewalk—as later implied by defense counsel—would create a laceration of the skin with irregular tearing margins as the skin is stretched at the moment of impact, not the sharp margins in most of the wounds, as seen in the photo.

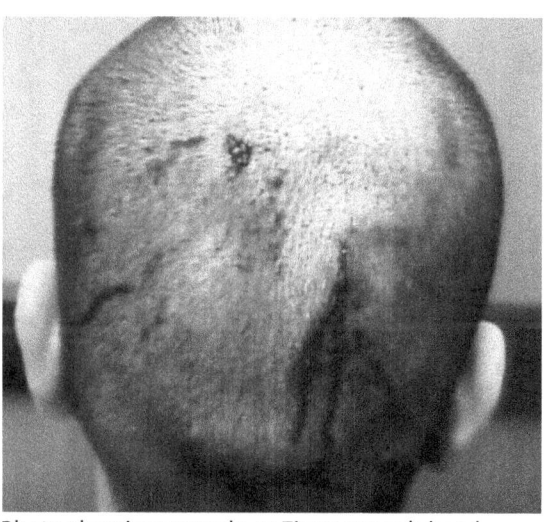

Photo showing wounds on Zimmerman's head.

The pattern here is much more characteristic of being impacted by a blunt object with only a small part of the object directly striking the skin and causing the smooth-margined lacerations.

In addition to creating an irregularly marginated laceration, impact with a hard flat surface will usually create an abrasion—or scrape—on the skin surrounding the actual tear. These areas will also be in contact with the surface at the moment of impact— a pattern of injury that is clearly absent in the photo taken of George Zimmerman.

While the photo caption represents that it was taken within three minutes of the shooting, clearly the picture was taken indoors and apparently after a portion of scalp hair had been removed to better visualize the lacerations. Probably after the shooter had been taken to the police station, and possibly after some type of medical treatment had been given.

Multiple attempts were made to procure the actual paramedic records to clarify the latter issue, but apparently those records no longer exist. Even though these types of medical records are typically stored electronically and can be maintained indefinitely.

In any event, all the lacerations are very superficial and quite obviously did not require any further medical care. Unlike most cases of deep scalp injury wherein irrigation and disinfection of the wound is required, and it is usually necessary to place sutures to approximate the margins and promote healing.

In the article on the next page references were made to the testimony of Dr. Di-Maio in which he indicates that there were several blows to the head—which would be consistent with the head being struck with some object while stationary. Not indicative of an individual's head being slammed into a concrete sidewalk multiple times, creating a moving head injury, often associated with significant consequential neurological damage and clinical symptomology.

DiMaio further opined that the injuries would have been serious, and the shooter should have been taken to the hospital. Conclusions not supported by the facts, considering the medical evaluation at the scene did not result in transport as a trauma alert.

It is not clear at this point, since there is no existing transcript from the trial, whether the testimony from DiMaio was challenged at all by the prosecutors during cross-examination— who should have obtained the EMS records for evaluation.

In Florida, prior to any criminal trial, it is routine for depositions to be taken of the various individuals, particularly medical experts, who might be called to testify in order that their opinions be documented.

Essentially this locks-in what issues can be brought up when that person is on the witness stand and eliminates the element of surprise—referred to as trial by ambush.

Clearly the prosecution was aware from deposition testimony, that Dr. DiMaio intended to address the injuries at trial, having previously presented the testimony of Dr. Valerie

Rao who'd indicated in earlier testimony for the State, that the injuries were not severe.

Both she and DiMaio appear to agree, however, that the injuries were consistent with a moving object striking the head—i.e., "blows"—and not a moving head striking a stationary object, which would most likely have been described by any forensic pathologist as "impacts."

The clear visual evidence, as well as testimony from their own medical expert—who characterized them as blows to the head, not impacts—would in no way support the assertion by the defense during closing arguments that there was multiple impacts with the head being repeatedly slammed against the cement sidewalk. This was dramatically demonstrated by the defense through the use of a mannequin, repeatedly slamming its head into the floor.

This demonstration by the defense attorney commenced with no apparent objection from the State, despite testimony from multiple experts including their own—indicating that this was not the mechanism of injury. A blow to the head is completely different than a head being pounded into a cement sidewalk.

The latter situation would involve the head, including the brain which floats free in liquid Cerebrospinal fluid within the interior of the skull, tethered only by the lower brain stem, being in motion—in the case of the scenario being depicted in this case, severe motion.

When this moving head suddenly decelerates upon impacting a stationary object such as a cement sidewalk, the brain can bounce around significantly, causing swelling and often bleeding in the subdural space between the brain and the skull. The result of this brain swelling can be a concussion or worse, with significant changes in the neurological status of the patient—both immediate and developing more slowly over a period of hours.

The latter situation is precisely the reason that head trauma patients are kept under medical observation for at least several hours to be sure these delayed symptoms don't develop—as the outcome could be fatal if not treated immediately. Clearly, examination of the shooter at the scene by the paramedics did not indicate that his wounds were significant enough to warrant such follow-up. In addition to the lack of the jagged-edged lacerations and the abrasions that would be expected to be imparted to the scalp during contact with the cement, Zimmerman showed little evidence of any neurological changes when evaluated by the paramedics at the scene.

Of equally critical importance among the other discrepancies is the absence of any swelling in the scalp that would be expected with trauma to the head, the goose-egg that most everyone has probably experienced themselves at some point in their lives.

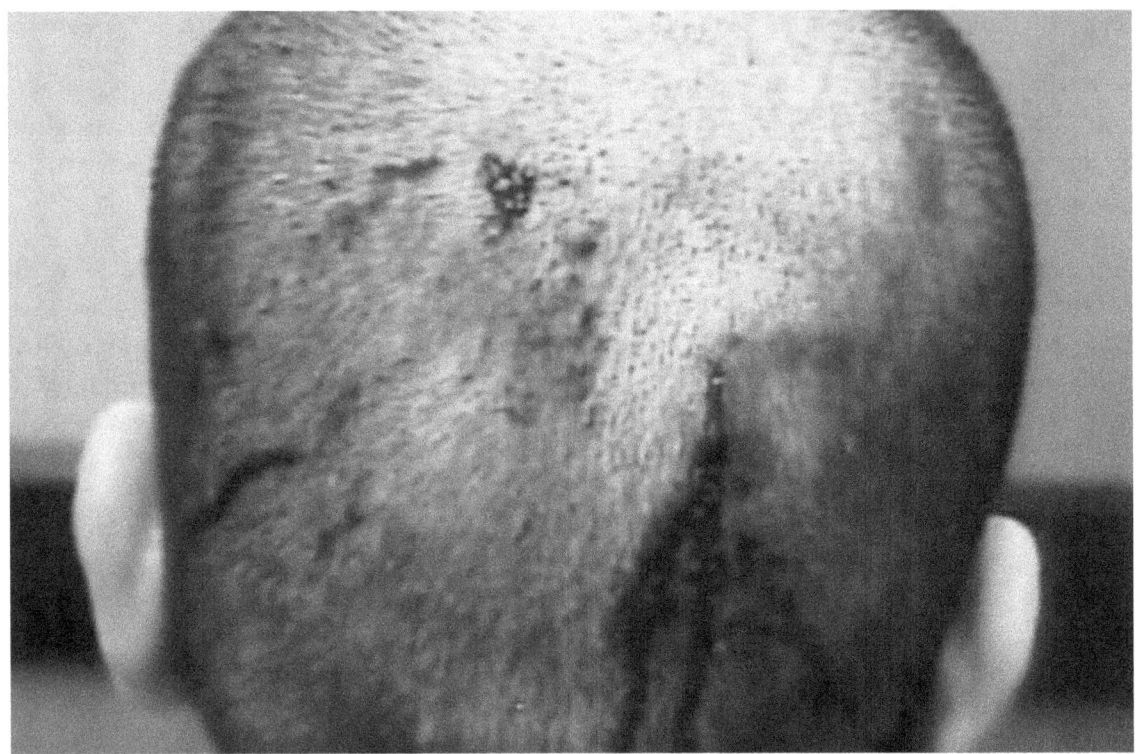

While the photos showed the wounds, it is important to note that there is no swelling or discoloration caused by an underlying hematoma that would have certainly developed if there had been repeated impacts with a cement sidewalk, as purported to have occurred by the defense counsel.

The score of 15 in the "Glasgow Coma Scale" described below that was applicable in this case indicates the absence of any significant head trauma either from direct impact or from a moving head injury and would be totally inconsistent with an individual having had his head repeatedly bashed against the sidewalk.

In fact, at the scene of the shooting, when the paramedics and police arrived within minutes, Mr. Zimmerman was evaluated and treated. The paramedic nurse cleaned up the two cuts on the back of Mr. Zimmerman's head. He declined any hospital treatment or examination. The pictures have shown that the minor cuts on the back of Mr. Zimmerman's head were superficial, thus, no hospitalization was required. More importantly, the nurse paramedic in attending to Mr. Zimmerman, evaluated him as a "perfect 15 on the Glasgow Coma Scale."

TRAYVON MARTIN CASE

Neighbor: Zimmerman pinned down

• WITNESSES, FROM 1A

— erupted after a controversial Instagram photo of Zimmerman defense attorney Don West and his daughters came to light.

Molly West, a 20-something daughter of West, posted the photo to her Instagram account. It showed her, her father and her sister eating Chick-fil-A ice cream cones Monday, with the caption: "We beat stupidity celebration cones" and the hashtag #dadkilledit. Don West had on Monday made a joke in his opening statement that some found insensitive.

As news of the photo rapidly spread, Molly West and her sister, Rachel, quietly left the courtroom for the day. Defense team spokesman Shawn Vincent said, Molly "is mortified ... for bringing negative attention to her father and the case." The Instagram account is now closed.

"Don had no idea that she'd post it on Instagram, and he also knew nothing about the comments associated with it," he said, acknowledging the bad taste and timing of the image. "We understand the context of the comments with what's happened in court this week are grossly insensitive."

He added: "Don told me, 'As a parent, we're not always proud of the things our children do, but we love them anyway, and then we move on.'"

In court Friday, a string of witnesses testified to what they saw or heard that night.

Good said he saw a "tussle" between Zimmerman and Trayvon a few feet from his patio and that he believed — based on the colors of clothes he saw — that Trayvon had pinned down Zimmerman on the ground.

Good was the first person to testify that he thought he saw Trayvon on top of Zimmerman, and that it was Zimmerman who may have been crying out for help from underneath. His testimony contradicts witness Selma Mora, now a Miami resident, who testified Thursday that she thought she saw Zimmerman on top during the scuffle.

Good stopped short, however, of saying that he saw the person on top throwing punches or slamming the other man's head on the sidewalk, as Zimmerman contends Trayvon did to him.

INSTAGRAM

ON INSTAGRAM: Defense lawyer Don West is seen with daughters Rachel, left, and Molly in the photo, captioned 'We beat stupidity celebration cones.'

Zimmerman, 29, has said he acted in self-defense, shooting Trayvon after the unarmed teen attacked him. Prosecutors say Zimmerman profiled and pursued Trayvon. He's charged with second-degree murder, which carries a penalty of up to life in prison if convicted.

The case sparked protests and marches in the 44 days between Trayvon's death and Zimmerman's arrest. It also led to vigorous debates about race and Florida's controversial Stand Your Ground law, which does not apply to this case.

A six-person, all-female jury, sequestered by Seminole County Circuit Judge Debra Nelson, will decide Zimmerman's fate.

Jurors on Friday also heard Smith, the first responding officer, testify about Zimmerman's demeanor and actions, noting that he was calm and followed officers' orders.

Another witness, Jonathan Manalo, a neighbor who was the first to speak with Zimmerman before officers arrived, said he seemed coherent but looked as if he had been in a fight.

"It looked to you like he had just got his butt beat?" defense attorney West asked.

"Yes," Manalo responded.

As Smith handcuffed Zimmerman, Manalo said, Zimmerman asked Manalo to call his wife, Shellie. Manalo said he dialed the number and began to explain that there had been a shooting and Zimmerman would be at the Sanford Police Department.

"Just tell her I shot some-

one," Manalo recalled an impatient Zimmerman saying.

Paramedic Stacey Livingston said she treated Zimmerman for "about five minutes" at the scene, cleaning up two cuts on the back of his head. She also noted that his nose was "very swollen" but Zimmerman declined to be taken to the hospital. She said she evaluated Zimmerman as a perfect 15 on the Glasgow Coma Scale, meaning his eyesight and verbal and motor skills were unimpaired.

A physician's assistant who examined Zimmerman the next day, Lindzee Folgate, told jurors that he complained of nose pain and displayed injuries consistent with being struck in the face and thrown to the ground.

But Folgate also said Zimmerman was not suffering from headaches, dizziness, numbness or blurred vision when she saw him. She said he had nausea at the thought of the shooting, which she determined to be psychological, not physiological.

Friday's testimony capped a dramatic week in a fifth-floor courtroom where jurors heard from 22 state witnesses in the opening week of testimony.

Prosecutor John Guy jolted jurors to attention in his opening statement Monday when he repeated expletives that Zimmerman can be heard saying on a recorded call when he phoned police to report a suspicious person a few minutes before the shooting. Zimmerman attorney West led his opening argument with a knock-knock joke that fell flat.

Graphic crime-scene images and emotional 911 calls with audible screams and a gunshot sent Trayvon's parents, often in tears, walking

out of the courtroom.

The longest and most-talked-about testimony so far has come from 19-year-old Miami student Rachel Jeantel, a childhood friend of Trayvon's who was speaking on the phone with him moments before his death.

She remained steadfast, even under intense cross-examination that stretched over two days, about what she heard on those final phone calls with Trayvon, including that she heard him say "Why are you following me for?" followed by "get off, get off." She acknowledged, however, that she could not say for sure who the aggressor was because she was not there.

Jeantel's testimony, like Molly West's Instagram photo, kicked up a storm of comments on Twitter, Facebook and other social media sites, where posters opined on everything from her appearance to her diction. The criticisms was followed by pushback from supporters who defended her and praised her courage.

The discovery of Molly West's Instagram photo came a day after O'Mara discussed the power of social media in the case. He said it was "amazing," adding that he had barely even heard of Twitter before he became Zimmerman's attorney last year.

The defense team launched a blog last year to document evidence and updates in the case and raise money. Supporters on both sides have used social media to release information and comments about the case long before the trial got under way.

"We've had witnesses walk out of the courtroom and start tweeting," O'Mara said.

COMFORTABLE FOR YOU AND YOUR WALLET

ALSO

• SAVE UP TO 56% ON YOUR ELECTRIC BILL
• 100% FINANCING LOW INTEREST AVAILABLE
• POTENTIAL FEDERAL TAX CREDIT
• FPL REIMBURSEMENTS
• 24X7 TECHNICAL SERVICE

GET UP TO $1,900* IN POTENTIAL REBATES

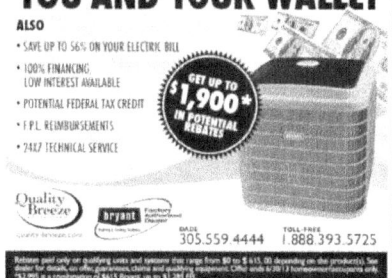

Quality Breeze   bryant

305.559.4444   TOLL-FREE 1.888.393.5725

The Glasgow Coma Scale is a clinical scale used to reliably measure a person's level of consciousness after a head injury. The test assesses the person's ability to perform eye movements, to speak, and to move parts of their body. These three behaviors then are scored and result in the ultimate numeric range. A score of 15 means that there is virtually nothing wrong with this person that would require further medical treatment and attention.

The Glasgow Coma Scale was developed by doctors at the University of Glasgow Medical School in 1974. This testing and evaluation are universally used to assist healthcare providers in measuring any decreases in consciousness or disruptions in nervous system function. It is most widely used to measure comas and decreases in consciousness. Based on the observations, testing, and the fact that Zimmerman was not suffering from any headache, dizziness, numbness, or blurred vision, he received a perfect 15.

This appears to be empirical evidence that Mr. Zimmerman's claim to be the assault victim after suffering such a severe attack that his shooting of this young man was justified is a bogus claim not based upon the forensic evidence.

The Prosecution in this case did not present evidence to the jury of what really was the cause of the alleged "injuries" to Mr. Zimmerman. This evaluation and the "perfect 15" on the Glasgow Coma Scale are totally inconsistent with the assertions by the Defense. This evaluation was done moments after the shooting and at the crime scene—not determined later by subsequent purported inquiries, changes in testimony by Mr. Zimmerman, or input from lawyers.

The unchallenged valuation by the on-scene paramedic not only impeaches the claim of the severe attack and justifications, but it also refutes Mr. Zimmerman's additional claims that he had been "punched 25 to 30 times" in addition to the head slamming on the sidewalk.

Yet, these clear discrepancies were not addressed, with the jurors left to consider only an unchallenged reconstruction of the event based solely upon the account provided by the defendant himself.

Jurors, who were instructed to consider only the evidence presented to them, would consequently arrive at a totally incorrect conclusion, completely contradictory to all the medical expert evidence. A contradiction that would not necessarily be evident to a lay person unless it was pointed out and fully explained to them.

Those contradictions certainly were not conveyed to them by the State Prosecutors—who seemed to show little interest in a more thorough examination of the forensic details of the case, even allowing the defendant's account of the incident to be tacitly accepted as factual. It is understandable that these details would not be brought up unilaterally by the Defense.

Because this demonstration was left unchallenged, the jurors would tend to accept this as a reliable recreation of events. An action that would significantly and materially affect their ultimate decision as to the guilt or innocence of the defendant.

The theory of the case for the defense, based upon self-defense in the face of threat of death or serious bodily injury was therefore also allowed to go essentially unchallenged. This resulted in a rather predictable verdict of "not guilty" from the jury, based upon the medical evidence presented to them.

Regarding the gunshot wound, the entire focus seems to have been on the proximity of the weapon, which was not even particularly consequential, but no witness apparently discussed or even discovered the discrepancies regarding the wound tract as we pointed out earlier.

If Martin, while on top of Zimmerman, had reached his right arm across his body while attempting to reach the gun supposedly on the latter's right hip area, Martin's chest would be significantly rotated to the left, resulting in a bullet entering left chest would have a right-to-left trajectory striking the left lung and possibly the tip of the left ventricle.

This is exactly the opposite directionality that is described in the autopsy report and what was presented to the jury as evidence by Dr. Bao.

It is incontrovertible evidence that the account of the incident videotaped by law enforcement and presented as fact to the jury throughout the trial, was totally incorrect. A bullet entering the left side of the chest subsequently striking the right ventricle of the heart and then the right lung is going left-to-right, not straight back.

We know from the office records that Dr. Bao was not a part of the re-enactment orchestrated by the police and featured Zimmerman clearly showing how Trayvon had reached across his body with the right hand attempting to grab the gun. A scenario created by the shooter himself, not conjecture or theory created by a third party, but the "facts" as created by the shooter.

It is puzzling as to why the police would even undertake such a reconstruction in this case. An action that has seldom, if ever been encountered by most medical examiners in cases of homicide—allowing the suspect to recreate the crime and then accepting the findings as fact—not to be challenged throughout the entire investigative and prosecution process.

It is further questionable as to whether Dr. Shiping Bao or Dr. Valarie Rao were, at any point ever apprised of the existence of the video re-enactment and certainly there is no evidence that she had the opportunity to analyze it.

While it is important for the pathologist not to be unduly influenced by information that might turn out to be erroneous while conducting a forensic autopsy, that does not apply to documented factual evidence — so called hard evidence—in the work-up of a forensic autopsy.

For the medical examiner who performed the autopsy and determined the path of the projectile not to be informed of such a critical piece of evidentiary data is beyond the scope of incompetence but strongly suggests a deliberate effort to create a situation wherein a determination of homicide could not be reached by a jury should the case ultimately be prosecuted.

Compounding the situation is the fact that while researching the issue of allowing the suspect to set the fact base himself by reconstructing the incident, no instances—particularly in Sanford Florida—were found or in memory wherein this had ever occurred.

It is unclear as to whether Dr. DiMaio had access to the video as part of his consultation on the case, but most likely would have discovered the discrepancies had he reviewed the purported reconstruction of the incident.

Screenshot taken from a YouTube video.

As a defense expert, however, this is information that would not be included in testimony unless directly asked about it by the attorneys from one side or the other.

Clearly the defense was not going to raise the issue unilaterally, as it would destroy the credibility of the video. It certainly would have required Zimmerman to take the stand personally and explain the contradictions between his account and the autopsy findings.

So long as the video was left unchallenged, there was no need for that to happen and risk subsequent cross-examination by the State. Again, the failure of the State prosecutors—who have access to virtually unlimited resources when it comes to criminalistic and forensic expertise—to recognize the problem with the reconstruction video and the factual data from the autopsy, stretches the limits of incompetency and points to a potential deliberate ignoring of the facts.

Even the most limited questioning of the validity of the account by the defendant would almost certainly have required his direct testimony to clarify the discrepancies. Thereby allowing the State to directly confront the defendant on the stand in front of the jury. Otherwise, the lynchpin of their defense, the video re-enactment, would essentially be out the window.

This apparently was not what the State was interested in doing in prosecuting the death of Trayvon Martin. Even when the defense expert was on the stand during cross-examination by the prosecution attorneys, all the discussion was related to the proximity of the weapon. Including soot on the clothing and the presence of stippling gunpowder effects on the skin. A factor of questionable significance in this case, because intentional homicides can occur at close range just as easily as self-defense wounds.

At no point was the issue of trajectory of the bullet wound path discussed to any extent during the cross-examination. Thereby keeping the jurors completely in the dark as to even the mere existence of any problems with the medical evidence presented to them for their deliberation.

Throughout the entire history of this unfortunate death, the truths that might have been ascertained by the proper gathering, analysis, and interpretation of scientific forensic evidence, were essentially ignored either thru ignorance, incompetence or intentional disregard. This was clearly the case if the factual data didn't support the hidden agendas of both the defense attorneys and the State prosecutors.

Within the supposedly unbiased and independent system of justice—particularly as relates to medico-legal death investigation— there exists an undercurrent of prejudice, bias and relatively-invisible political influence that belies the popular theme of TV show's portrayal that is presented to the public as reality.

When a totally unsubstantiated video re-enactment of a crime, authored by the perpetrator, is introduced by the State as factual evidence to the jury, it is understandable that that evidence would be accepted as true.

Remember, the jurors are instructed to confine their deliberations to the evidence presented to them at trial, and only that evidence, when arriving at their ultimate verdict of guilty or not guilty.

Zimmerman says that the victim, Trayvon, attacked him, got him on the ground and repeatedly bashed his head against the sidewalk. He also claimed that it made him feel as though his head was exploding and the Defense attempted to assert that his claim of self-defense was to save his own life.

It is during this alleged, but unwitnessed, detailed struggle that Mr. Zimmerman claims that Trayvon tried to reach Zimmerman's gun but was "beat to the draw" and shot.

Notably, it was the lead Prosecutor who initially brought out the dummy and in front of the jury, placed himself on top of it laying on the floor.

It is not clear why he felt he needed to introduce these theatrics as evidence as it would confirm this sequence of events in the minds of the jurors who, trusting the State to present substantiated evidence, would assume it to be the truth.

Nothing about this fiasco could be further from the truth as determined from the actual scientific forensic analyses.

To make matters worse, it allowed the defense to have access to the dummy in the process subsequently used to reinforce the erroneous assumption that Trayvon was on top of Zimmerman when the fatal shot was fired.

This then allowed a basis for defense counsel O'Mara to "demonstrate" in the middle of the courtroom to the jury the alleged attack against defendant Zimmerman.

Mr. O'Mara was allowed to straddle an inflated dummy and illustrate his concept of grabbing and repeatedly hitting its head against the sidewalk. As we now know that did not happen and it obviously was an intentional fabrication brought up by the defense to try to justify the murder.

There were many similar errors made in the presentation of this case. One must wonder whether the errors or omissions were intentionally made to assure an acquittal. Or were the errors negligently and incompetently made by a prosecution that did not have the appropriate expertise and experience?

The truth is that this prosecution team did have significant trial experience in the prosecution of similar cases. The question then as to what happened and why has not been answered.

It should be remembered that contrary to all common sense in the defense of criminal cases, the defendant Zimmerman was allowed to create a one-man-show of him being filmed reenacting what he claimed had happened on that evening.

There were so many things revealed by his dramatic presentation that were inconsistent with the rest of the evidence, one must wonder why it was even presented to the jury.

The State chose to introduce to the jury the Zimmerman reenactment. Had they not done so, Zimmerman would have had no choice but to take the stand as a witness and testify if the forensic evidence been properly analyzed and interpreted.

That of course would have subjected him to lengthy and vigorous examinations as to numerous details. Not only that, but it would have also opened him up clearly to being exposed for all his changes in testimony and outright lies.

Throughout the litigation the defense wisely and expertly played it coy. They allowed the prosecution and news media to "assume" that they would present a defense of "Stand Your Ground" thus making it necessary for Zimmerman to testify.

Likewise, it is difficult to understand how these errors could have happened. Two of the prosecutors in the case were experienced and successful criminal trial lawyers.

Similarly, the defense lawyers were both Board Certified and recognized as experts. One might reasonably speculate that there were simply too many mistakes to entirely eliminate the possibility that they weren't accidental.

From the first actions at the scene, major mistakes were made eliminating the possibility to gather important forensic evidence. This included loss of DNA and fibers from Trayvon's hands by taking totally unnecessary fingerprints to run through a criminal database, and not bothering to attend the autopsy in order to get the forensic data about the wounds.

Then continuing forward with allowing the potential defendant to recreate a self-serving video recording of his version of events, that was used as evidence in the trial.

Thus, inexplicably allowing that fabrication that was completely unsupported by a proper interpretation of the forensic evidence to become a key factor in the trial.

This key error allowed the unchallenged presentation by the defense to demonstrate the mechanism through which the wounds to the head of the shooter were imparted.

One could also be excused from mistaking this operation as an episode of the Keystone Cops or Reno 911, not a homicide investigation conducted by a professional Police Department and Prosecutor for the State of Florida!

Epilogues

EPILOGUE — J. CHENEY MASON

It is very common to hear phrases and references regarding the police, in general, as having a "blue wall." This is referenced commonly in movies, television shows, and true crime thrillers. The first actions of the police at the crime scene revealed some apparent prejudice in favor of the admitted shooter. He was identified from the beginning as a kind of official Neighborhood Watch commander. It is obvious that the officers treated him from the beginning as the victim, not the aggressor.

First, after Mr. Zimmerman related his spontaneous story alleging the severe injuries to himself that are highly suspect, the police appeared to have given him the benefit of any, if not all, doubt. In fact, during the evening and continuing investigation, there were witnesses that severely impeached the claims by Mr. Zimmerman.

There were at least eight calls on 911 reporting to the police hearing the "cries for help," many opining that they were from a young person. The fact is that immediately after the single shot the "cries for help" stopped. An important witness testified that she not only heard, but also saw, what conveyed through body language the appearance of the shooter flailing his arms over his head as if to convey that he had really messed up. Not only did this witness advise the same, but so did her roommate.

Nevertheless, the police chose to ignore them and rather simply accept as "fact" the improbable claims by Mr. Zimmerman. When all is reviewed of the scene and claims by the shooter, and one considers the numerous major changes in his story, it seems only reasonable to conclude that the police simply deferred to the "Watch Commander," regardless of the inconsistencies and contradicting forensic evidence.

The State Attorney in charge of the circuit including Seminole County, Mr. Norm Wolfinger, had a history of supporting improbable but favorable to the police side of stories in multiple cases. When we review and consider the fact of the shooting here, as simple as it was, to not even arrest Mr. Zimmerman and make no efforts to do so for a long time raises at least some reasonable doubt.

Remember that in accordance with all the reports in multiple newspapers and journals, the State Attorney publicly declared support for the position of Police Chief Lee who stated he did not think there was "probable cause" to make an arrest or bring charges against Mr. Zimmerman.

This is the same State Attorney who was instrumental in the wrongful conviction years earlier of Mr. Wilton Dedge. Dedge had been convicted in two trials with Appellate reversals by the State Attorney presenting such suspect evidence as to be unbelievable. In the Dedge case, a rape by described assailant of being 6'2" tall and over 200 pounds resulted in the conviction of Mr. Dedge who was 5'6" and 130 pounds.

It also resulted in presenting the evidence by a retired police officer that he had a tracking dog capable of following human scents not only as late as eight years after the fact, and even through water.

This type of "junk-science" has unfortunately persisted despite being utterly debunked by virtually every credible organization of forensic science. The reason for this persistence is that in virtually all instances the "evidence" that is created, regardless of any scientific validity, can be used successfully in the prosecution or defense of the case in point.

That police witness and questionable evidence resulted in wrongful convictions and ultimate exoneration of at least fifteen people. Those incredible injustices had been fully revealed and were known to Mr. Wolfinger at the time of the killing of Trayvon Martin.

After the exoneration of Mr. Dedge, there was continued public outcry seeking investigations of the corruption within this State Attorney's Office and State Attorney.

This continued for more than a decade after the full exoneration of Mr. Dedge and resulted in a false promise by the Florida Attorney General at the time, Ms. Pam Bondi. She promised a full and complete investigation of the apparent prejudices and corruption in the State Attorney's Office, which did not happen.

EPILOGUE — WILLIAM R. ANDERSON, M.D.

Throughout the vast majority of human history, legal judgments have been based upon totally erroneous theories and assumptions that led to preposterous outcomes such as deciding whether or not an accused was a witch based upon whether she would float or sink when thrown into a vat filled with water. Or burning the hands with a hot iron and determining innocence of guilt on whether or not the wound healed properly—an unlikely event in the pre-antibiotic Middle Ages.

Countless individuals, often completely innocent, have been imprisoned, tortured, and even executed because of these "theories" which appear to be ridiculous to us now, but were firmly-held beliefs at the time.

In the late 19th and early 20th Centuries, the focus was on the development of the various scientific methods that would aid in the analysis of data that could be considered as evidence both in the areas of criminalistics, as well as the medical sciences. This afforded scientific information to be used to find and prosecute perpetrators of unlawful activities, as well as avoiding wrongful accusations and, in the worst-case scenario, convictions of innocent subjects.

The promise that the interjection of science with its perceived inherent precision and objectivity to the justice system would bring results that were more accurate and equitable, has in many ways been fulfilled. However, because of the human-factors that are involved in the process, those hopes may not always be realized.

Because any scientific analysis involves human beings as part of the process, a certain amount of subjectivity is invariably involved both in the gathering and processing of that 'evidence', and the ultimate interpretations as to what the results meant, relative to the particular case at hand.

At a crime scene, evidence must be collected and submitted to the lab before it can be tested. If certain pieces of potential data are not gathered because an investigator decides it doesn't fit into some preconceived theory that has been postulated relative to that crime—potential evidence pointing in another direction may be ignored. This could result in evidence being deemed unimportant even though it could possibly point to another suspect.

During the prosecution of a case, the attorneys may choose to ignore, or even attempt to hide, evidence that was collected and analyzed but may be exculpatory (proving inno-cense) as regards their suspect, or even point to another person. Deciding that winning the case would be better politically than admitting they were prosecuting the wrong person.

The challenge today is to bring public attention the potential pitfalls that may be encountered when medical science interacts with the legal system. Particularly as the presentation of scientific data is almost expected by jurors in any criminal or civil trial wherein such information is, or should be, reliable, understandable, and available.

Indeed, the attorneys on either side of a case may suffer negative consequences if the jurors feel evidence has either been mishandled or not presented in good faith.

Consequently, it is the duty of the forensic scientist—including the practitioners of forensic medicine—to ensure that this type of misrepresentation whether inadvertent or intentional, never happens.

The traditional function of the forensic pathologist/Medical Examiner was to deal with deaths that occurred suddenly, unexpectedly, under suspicious circumstances, or as the result of any type of trauma, and to determine the cause of the death, as well as the manner—whether it was a natural death, or the result of accident, suicide, or homicide.

In the best of all worlds, this determination would be made by the pathologist, based upon the actual autopsy findings, and independent of any outside influences.

The reality is quite different, however, with the police often providing information of the event that was biased toward their take on the case, the Prosecution insisting that the Medical Examiner being a part of the prosecutorial team, with pressure being applied subtly that too many disagreements could have an effect on job security, and the politicians who would ignore the needs of the office in its routine functions to the point of neglect. Only to become intrusive when a death was the result some situation that could provide a potential for liability or embarrassment.

This was the quandary faced by many forensic pathologists who, while having strong ethical and moral values that insisted that the truth should prevail, were under the constant specter of potential career damage if they were too forceful in resisting their employer—the Government—in providing support in medicolegal situations, even though the science didn't support their position.

Any Forensic Pathologist, particularly one who's a stickler for scientific integrity, most likely would have on more than a few occasions butted heads with the politicians, elected officials and other authorities in the County—including the administration and the police, over decisions he or she had made.

This usually results when the autopsy findings didn't support either the investigator's theory of what supposedly happened to cause the death of the person or persons in question, or the attorney's basis for a criminal prosecution.

The dichotomy that exists in this case is between the usual close relationship that exists between the forensic scientist and the prosecutorial agencies in cases involving potential homicide, and what actually transpired in the investigation and management of the case involving the death of Trayvon Martin.

The individuals analyzing and interpreting the wounds on the body, including the determination of range, trajectory, extent of internal injuries, and injury patterns—factors critical in arriving at a proper and objective conclusion—were not apparently involved at all in most of the investigative activities.

The cascading number of errors, either of commission or omission, begins to stretch the credibility of a conclusion of simple incompetence. Particularly considering the caliber of the attorneys involved, and rather points to the unmistakable conclusion that these actions were deliberate, either at the overt or subconscious level.

Had a more thorough investigation of the gunshot trajectory been made, the fact that scientific evidence clearly refuted the video-taped reenactment of the incident purported by the shooter, it would most-likely have been discovered.

Had Dr. Bao even been apprised that the video was being created—well in advance of any autopsy findings had been released—or even aware of the existence of said video, the error may also have been discovered and rectified, long before being presented to the jury as a true account of the shooting.

This afforded the opportunity for the investigation, clearly tainted with bias and prejudice, to go forward unabated until public pressure finally forced the authorities to advance prosecution—still placing the forensic evidence on the back burner.

The Medical Examiner had, according to the available records, virtually no interaction with the prosecutors of the case until the eve of the trial. At no point in the entire case was the discrepancy with the trajectory of the bullet ever addressed.

To the contrary, the Prosecutors accepted the video account as fact and themselves presented that fact to the jury.

The two forensic pathologists offered to the jury by the Prosecution, Dr. Shiping Bao, and Dr. Valerie Rao discussed the distance of the gun from the body and the head wounds observed on the shooter, respectively. Nothing was included about the trajectory of the bullet.

Defense expert Dr. Vince DiMaio also testified about the same things Dr. Bao had covered but was predictably not asked about trajectory during the Defense presentation, and despite their opportunity during cross-examination, by the State Attorney.

Instead, DiMaio gave testimony regarding Zimmerman's head injuries, contradicting both Dr. Rao and clear medical evidence, while indicating that the wounds were severe and even potentially life threatening.

This misconception and mischaracterization were later fortified when the Defense was allowed, without objection, to provide a visual demonstration. Wherein the head of a dummy, previously used by the Prosecutor to show Trayvon on top of the shooter, was used in a move that reinforced the notion that the video account was accurate to repeatedly bang the dummy's head into the floor.

The lack of either an objection by the Prosecutor pointing out that there was no medical evidence to support the notion advanced by Defense, or at least a later explanation to the jury clarifying the issue, allowed that image to be implanted in their minds as truth.

This truth was then carried with them back to the jury room.

As we stated earlier: "Fiction becomes fact...facts disappear."

And in the process: Truth disappears as well.

What's your verdict?

Authors' Biographies

J. CHENEY MASON

Mr. Mason has been an active trial lawyer for approximately 54 years. He graduated from the University of Florida College of Law in 1970 and began private law practice in Orlando, Florida. He specializes in criminal defense and marital and family law. He is Board Certified as a criminal trial law specialist by both the Florida Bar and the National Board of Trial Advocacy.

Mr. Mason's career includes numerous high-profile cases. His first trial in a First-Degree Murder case was in 1972. The most notorious murder case was as the senior counsel defending Casey Anthony in her sensational trial in 2011 and he has tried six First Degree Murder Trials since then.

Among other high-profile cases was the successful criminal defense trial of Miami Police Major Aaron Campbell who had been profile stopped and wrongfully prosecuted, resulting in the frequently thereafter used mantra "Driving While Black." Mr. Mason has presented jury trials in an estimated 350 cases over the last 54 years, many of which have essentially become the "history" in criminal law quarters.

He is the recipient of numerous awards from a variety of professional organizations including being awarded the highest professional award by the National Association of Criminal Defense Lawyers, the "Heeney Award," received in 2004. He served as an NGO Delegate to the United Nations in Vienna, Austria representing the National Association of Criminal Defense Lawyers in the International Symposium on Human Trafficking. He also received the highest award annually bestowed by the Florida Association of Criminal Defense Lawyers, the Goldstein Award, presented in 2022.

He has authored and published a book about the Casey Anthony case, "Justice in America: How Prosecutors and the Media Conspire Against the Accused." Additionally, he recently published a book about prostate cancer, "Facing and Surviving Prostate Cancer Today."

Mr. Mason has been a primary participant in multiple Netflix presentations and numerous nationally publicized critiques and evaluations of major criminal trials. He has been a prominent speaker in criminal law seminars in multiple states and jurisdictions. Mr. Mason has also made guest appearances in numerous national television shows.

He is an U.S. Air Force Veteran having served 3 years in the Far East and Southeast Asia. He is a father of 2, grandfather of 7, and currently 5 great grandchildren.

DR WILLIAM ANDERSON

Dr. William R. Anderson was awarded his Medical Doctor's degree in 1968 from the University of Miami. He received his Residency Training at Strong Memorial Hospital University of Rochester, School of Medicine from 1968-1970 in Anatomic Pathology. He received additional training in Cardiac and Clinical Pathology from 1973-1974 at Duke University School of Medicine. He also studied Forensic and Clinical Pathology at the University of North Carolina School of Medicine at Chapel Hill from 1974-1976. He has been certified by the American Board of Pathology in 1976 in Anatomic & Forensic Pathology and in 1980 in Clinical Pathology.

His Professional experience includes serving as a Submarine & Diving Medical Officer, US Navy (1970-1972), Assistant Chief Medical Examiner, North Carolina (1974-1976), County Medical Examiner, Durham, N.C. (1973-1974), Associate to the Chief Medical Examiner, Los Angeles, Ca. (1976-1977), Medical Examiner, Cobb & DeKalb Counties, GA (1977-1979), Pathologist & Laboratory Director, Diagnostic Pathology Associates, Atlanta, Ga. (1979-1986). (Anatomic, Clinical & Forensic pathology services to a network of hospitals in north Georgia; director of clinical chemistry), Medical Director & Pathologist, International Clinical Laboratories, Syosset, NY (1986-1987), Forensic Pathologist and Consultant in Pathology & Legal Medicine, Atlanta, GA (1979-1990); (consultant to the Office of the Medical Examiner, Cobb & DeKalb Counties), Consultant in Forensic Pathology & Legal Medicine, (1988-present), Associate Medical Examiner, Collier County, FL; Coroner's Pathologist, Naperville, IL (1988-1990), Consultant in Medical Hazardous Waste Management: Scientific Waste Systems, Atlanta, GA, Deputy Chief Medical Examiner, District 9, Orlando, FL (1990-2002), Medical consultant, Orange County, FL., sexual battery evaluation & treatment, and analysis of injury patterns in child abuse cases (1990-2000), Surgical Pathology & Laboratory Director, Orange County Medical Clinic (1991-1994), Co-Director of Medical Education in Forensic Medicine, Orlando Region al Healthcare System—Trauma Surgery & Emergency Medicine (1991-2002), Director of Forensic Pathology Post-Graduate Training Program, Office of the Medical Examiner, District 9, Orlando, FL (1991-1998), Expert Witness Consultant Program, Dept. of Professional Regulation, State of Florida (1992-present), Pathologist Consultant & Autopsy Service: Central Florida Tissue Bank & TransLife Tissue Bank, Orlando, FL (1992-2004), Pathologist, Office of the Medical Examiner, District 12, Sarasota, FL (2002-2003), Forensic Pathologist, Forensic Dimensions, Orlando, FL (2003-present).

As Associate and Chief Medical Examiner in North Carolina, California, Georgia, & Florida, Dr. Anderson has performed over 7000 autopsy and clinical patient examinations in medicolegal cases and has been involved in testimony in over 300 cases in both the criminal and civil justice system.

BIBLIOGRAPHY

In every criminal trial in Florida, all proceedings in court are officially recorded by court reporters/stenographers. However, no printed copy of the proceedings/testimony will be prepared unless they are ordered by one of the parties and paid for. If a Defendant is convicted and thereafter seeks an Appeal, then there will be a complete printed transcript of the court proceedings as requested by either the defense, the prosecution, or both. Where the Defendant is found not guilty, then there is no Appeal and no need for a transcript of what actually happened in court, except in potentially unusual circumstances. In the case regarding the killing of Trayvon Martin, the Defendant, George Zimmerman, was found not guilty by the jury and therefore no Appeal. The following obvious result of that is there is no transcript available for anyone to read and, thus, confirm or impeach claimed statements or proceedings.

In our efforts to present the case in this book we, not having a transcript of the trial, had to rely on witnesses, court documents, and scientific evidence admitted in the proceedings. Accordingly, we were able to obtain and review all of the documents and exhibits relating to the cause and manner of death of Trayvon Martin, including the complete autopsy, photographs, diagrams, and sketches.

In order to attempt the most objective and corroborated statements regarding evidence from witnesses, we reviewed the newspaper and journal writings about the proceedings. While it is almost universally true that news reports or proceedings inherently are influenced by opinions of the journalists/writers, they can be essentially corroborated where there are numerous journalists revealing and writing about the same subject.

In this case, we reviewed in excess of 11,500 printed newspaper articles and articles from journals. The following is a list of those newspapers/journals that yielded this incredible volume. Every article was reviewed, and the subject matters and contents corroborated by the multiple disclosures, rather than any one or two journalists. The list of sources is below:

- The Orlando Sentinel
- Bradenton Herald
- Miami Herald
- Tallahassee Democrat
- South Florida Sun Sentinel
- Palm Beach Post
- Port Charlotte Sun
- Tampa Bay Times
- Pensacola News Journal
- The Stuart News

- Naples Daily News
- News Press
- Press Journal
- Rest in Power: The Trayvon Martin Documentary Series on Amazon Prime Video
- The report of autopsy and all supporting documents were obtained from the official records of the court file.
- Documents Quoted In Legal Analysis
- Constitution of the State of Florida, Article IV – Executive
- Constitution of the State of Florida, Article V – Judiciary